Adventures of A DEAN

A PRIMER ON BUSINESS SCHOOL MANAGEMENT

First Edition

By Dr. Howard Frank
University of Maryland

cognella
academic publishing
www.cognella.com   800-200-3908

Bassim Hamadeh, CEO and Publisher
Christopher Foster, General Vice President
Michael Simpson, Vice President of Acquisitions
Jessica Knott, Managing Editor
Stephen Milano, Creative Director
Kevin Fahey, Cognella Marketing Program Manager
Melissa Barcomb, Acquisitions Editor
Sarah Wheeler, Project Editor
Stephanie Sandler, Licensing Associate

First published in the United States of America in 2012 by University Readers, Inc.

Trademark Notice: Product or corporate names may be trademarks or registered trademarks, and are used only for identification and explanation without intent to infringe.

16 15 14 13 12   1 2 3 4 5

Printed in the United States of America

ISBN: 978-1-62131-529-2 (pbk) / 978-1-60927-553-2 (br)

Contents

Dedication

To my wife Jane who was an enormous help in developing this book, and more importantly, surviving the eleven years of my deanship.

Chapter One

Introduction

I quit four times before I finally quit. The first time I didn't quit, I had a meeting with the university's provost (the senior vice president and chief academic officer) to challenge an arbitrary decision he had made about canceling one of my projects. I went into the meeting carrying my resignation letter in my breast pocket, fully prepared to quit if he didn't reverse his position. After a heated argument, he conceded. But in return, I had to sign a document guaranteeing that I would pay $100,000 of the school's commitment if the school couldn't raise the money needed for my project.

Here is an extract from that resignation letter:

> This letter constitutes my resignation from the position of dean of the Robert H. Smith School of Business, effective January 1, 2004 ... Unfortunately, I have become convinced that the university no longer provides the entrepreneurial or management environment that would enable me to continue as dean. In particular, I have become increasingly frustrated by actions that I consider unfair, arbitrary, micromanagement, incompetent or biased. The university's decision to block the efforts of our alums to help us in funds raising by providing an appropriate development activity at the Comcast Center is the proverbial "straw that broke the camel's back." This action has damaged my ability to lead the school, will damage our relationships with our external supporters and has damaged the morale of my staff. This self-inflicted blow, when coupled with insensitive personnel and administrative

policies and budget cuts that I believe fell disproportionately on the business school, is no longer tolerable to me.

The second time I was ready to quit, but didn't, I was irate over two decisions the university had made that would cost the business school several million dollars. Here's an extract from my second undelivered letter of resignation:

> This letter constitutes my resignation from the position of dean of the Robert H. Smith School of Business, effective June 30, 2004 ... Unfortunately, I have become convinced that the university no longer provides the environment that would enable me to continue as dean. In particular, I have become increasingly frustrated by actions that I consider unfair, arbitrary, and biased against the business school. The recent decision to eliminate tuition remission on graduate fellowships not funded by the graduate school is the proverbial "straw that broke the camel's back." This action, coupled with your direction to prepare for another 1% budget cut, will cost the business school over $1 million. It will severely damage the quality of our MBA program, hurt our efforts to improve our external rankings, and damage the morale of my staff. This self-inflicted blow, when coupled with budget cuts that I believe fell disproportionately on the business school, is no longer tolerable to me."

This time, and after some wrangling, I was able to extract payments of $500,000 per year for five years to offset graduate student costs. Because the budget cuts costs us over one million dollars per year, we were in effect paying for that concession out of our own funds!

As time went on, it became easier for me to write a letter of resignation over some important issue and then not quit. I don't remember what caused me to write the third letter or why I decided not to deliver it, but here it is:

This letter constitutes my resignation from the position of dean of the Robert H. Smith School of Business, effective December 31, 2006 ... Unfortunately, I have become convinced that the university does not provide the entrepreneurial or management environment that would enable me to continue as dean. I have become increasingly frustrated by actions that I consider unfair, arbitrary, incompetent or biased. During the last nine years I have invested my time and spirit in the service of the business school. The result seems to be frequent damaging interactions with the rest of the campus. Rules seem to be created "after the fact" that hamper my ability to lead the school. The university promotes the idea of becoming a risk-taking entrepreneurial, global university less dependent on State support but its actions are anything but risk taking and entrepreneurial. Building the Smith School has been a constant battle against the university bureaucracy that I am no longer prepared to continue."

On the fourth try, I really did quit. The events leading to my resignation started with a series of e-mails with the provost that ended with this one, from me:

If your goal is to induce me to step down by insulting me, you have succeeded. You will be receiving my letter vacating the dean's position as of August 31, 2007.

And here is part of that letter, one I actually delivered to the provost and to the president:

With these facts, one would assume that the Smith School is an important asset to the University of Maryland. Therefore, it has become increasingly disturbing—and then shocking—for me to discover how little help senior administrators are willing to provide, and how disliked we are for what we have accomplished. I am also troubled by the great gap between University words and actions. For example, we have been encouraged to set up graduate programs in China. The University refused to assist us in setting up these operations and even declined to assemble a "lessons learned" team to benefit other schools seeking to expand internationally.

Although we have constantly pointed out the disjunct between global requirements and the University's domestically oriented graduate admission polices and practices, there have been no changes. We've made it very clear that without appropriate adjustments, our China operations are at risk. There does not appear to be much concern by the administration, but I'm sure that there would be if we took unilateral actions to close these operations.

With regard to unilateral operations, it is also shocking to me that you, as Provost, are quick to take unilateral action in an area such as MBA fees, without discussing these with me or with seemingly little regard for the consequences of this action. Also, while we've operated openly with your full approval, you've accused me of "misleading (at best)" students. I also don't see a reason for your insult but since this not the first time you have insulted me (only to later apologize), I accept this as part of your normal operating style. If you wanted my resignation, you should simply have asked for it since I serve as dean at your pleasure.

This letter is my formal notification to you that I will be vacating my deanship and returning to my faculty position effective September 1, 2007 ..."

A few days after delivering this letter I received a call from the president at my home at night asking me to meet with him to discuss my resignation. In that meeting he described what he called "a possible scenario," which went something like this:

The president's office will get petitions from students and faculty, there may be sit-ins, the newspapers will hear about it, there will be negative articles, people here will be interviewed and to defend themselves, they will say nasty things about you. It will be a mess. (Sidenote: I didn't know that he had already received a petition from our most senior faculty!) *On the other hand,* if you withdraw your resignation and resign a year from now, we will celebrate you, say great things, give you parties, and treat you the way you deserve to be treated.

My response: "I will withdraw my resignation."

Yes, I *withdrew* my resignation; but a year was asking for too much. About six months later, I submitted a new, and much longer (and nicer) letter:

Dear faculty and staff of the Smith School:

The time has come for me to announce that on June 30, 2008, I will be stepping down as dean of the Robert H. Smith School of Business.

When I joined the school in September 1997, the College of Business and Management was a small regional school with little recognition. The faculty and staff were excellent but small and overworked, and research was limited because of high teaching loads. The college's endowment stood at just $6 million, outreach to alumni was lacking, and we needed more space.

I was contacted in 1997 by the search committee to compete for the dean's position. The position description called for the new dean to, among other things,

- Significantly enhance the recognition and standing of the college,
- Continuously improve the college's academic programs and national prominence,
- Promote change and integrate it into the enduring culture of the college,

- Attract and recruit high caliber students and faculty,
- Recognize the importance of globalization and increase participation in the global arena, and
- Appreciate the growing importance of information technology in business and education.

Ten years after these directions were set, the college, now known as the Robert H. Smith School of Business, is a very different institution. Our students are terrific and are the pride of the campus. Our undergraduates have the highest SAT scores and the highest retention and graduation rates on campus. Teaching quality is superb.

Our graduate programs are the finest in the region and among the best in the world. The MBA and PhD programs are models of excellence on campus with graduation rates and times to graduation among the best at the university. The school, in accordance with campus strategy, has expanded its presence globally with numerous partners and programs. The Smith School dominates MBA education in the region with operations in College Park, Baltimore, Shady Grove and Washington, D.C. We've decreased teaching loads for PhD students, improved their research productivity and placement and increased their stipends when compared to other campus PhD students.

The school has achieved regional, national and international prominence. All of our programs have at least one top 20 ranking. On the information technology front, our rankings are in the top five in both research and programs. The Smith School has become one of the world's greatest research schools, currently ranked #5 in the world in research, surpassing every other public business school. This has been a colossal achievement since in 1996 it was rated #68.

Financially, the school has been prospering. Its revenues have quadrupled to more than $60 million per year. In every recent year, the school has operated at a surplus.

This surplus has been dedicated to improving services and facilities for our students. The faculty has nearly doubled in size. Van Munching Hall was expanded in 2002 and is again being expanded in 2007. The original Van Munching Hall was renovated in 2005. Today, more than 90% of our students study in an expanded and renovated Van Munching Hall, with leading-edge technology and state-of-the-art teaching laboratories. The new North Wing will help bring our remaining outside classrooms into Van Munching Hall. The school's endowment exceeds $50 million with more than an additional $45 million of gifts already committed during the new campaign.

The Smith School example is used by the university to illustrate what an entrepreneurial institution can accomplish. President Mote has led literally dozens of groups of state legislators through Smith School facilities, pointing with pride to what we've done and how we've done it with *minimal* state cost. Nearly all of these accomplishments stem from the efforts of our fabulous faculty, staff, alumni and friends of the school. We owe special debts of gratitude to Bob Smith, Leo Van Munching and a number of our alumni who have stepped up to the challenge of supporting the school during this critical growth phase.

While our ascent has not been flawless or mistake free, the university has benefited by the rising quality and reputation of the Smith School. Last year, the Smith School generated nearly 19% of the degrees awarded by the campus and the Smith School of Business has become a source of pride for the campus and indeed, the entire University System of Maryland.

It's certainly with mixed feelings that I am stepping down from my deanship. I look back with great pride on what has been accomplished during my tenure but I recognize that the school still has a way to go before it reaches our goal of being among the world's greatest business schools.

My plan is to begin a sabbatical on July 1, 2008 and then to return to the school as Professor of Management Sciences after the summer of 2009. The provost will be appointing a search committee for the next dean early in the fall semester. Given the school's strong competitive position, you can be sure that we will be able to attract a wonderful set of candidates for the next Smith School dean.

I have met many fine people here at the University of Maryland and am looking forward to helping the future growth and prosperity of the school and the university.

My tenure as dean was marked by extraordinary changes to the school, made all the more extraordinary because the university was a slow, conservative bureaucracy dedicated to halting—if not *crushing*—change. So, how did I get these changes to happen? Why did I stay for eleven years? Why did I leave? What did I learn? What more needs to be done? I wrote this book to answer those questions.

My Background

I was born on June 4, 1941, in the Bronx, the youngest of two children of working class parents. I attended junior high school in one of two "special progress (SP)" classes in the Bronx, so I was able to skip the eighth grade. I went on to Stuyvesant High School, one of the three original specialized public high schools in New York City, and the one that specialized in engineering and mathematics. I was a good, but not great, student except in plane geometry, where I excelled.

I attended the University of Miami (Florida) because it offered me a full scholarship, and I graduated first in my class with a BSEE degree in 1962. By that time I also had gotten a taste of what it meant to participate in college activities; I was editor of the engineering magazine, vice president of the local chapter of the IEEE (Institute of Electrical and Electronics Engineers), and vice president of engineering student government. From Miami I went directly to Northwestern

University (Illinois), this time on a fellowship. I received my MS in 1964, fell in love with graph theory, and decided to stay on for a Ph.D. in Electrical Engineering just so I could continue working in that area. At Northwestern I was recognized as one of their leading PhD students, and I completed my degree in 1965 in the minimum possible time: three years.

It was also an unusual three years. For, during that time I became good friends with my advisor. As of this writing, he is professor emeritus of mathematics at Northwestern, but back in 1964 we both dated music students and would frequently double date. I worked with him on research grants during the summers, and by the time I graduated we had already co-authored several research papers.

My plan was to go into the space industry after graduating, but my advisor contacted the head of the Electrical Engineering and Computer Sciences department at the University of California—Berkeley, and I was invited for an interview. They made me a job offer, I accepted, and two weeks after earning my PhD I headed west to begin my career as an Assistant Professor. In 1965, I was the youngest faculty member on the Berkeley campus.

I was a very productive researcher at Berkeley, authoring about 30 papers in my first three years. It was also to be a relatively short stint, for I was a member of Berkeley's faculty only from 1965–1970. I spent 1968–69 on leave as a full-time consultant within the Executive Office of the President of the United States. That invitation came about in a strange way, and it completely changed my career trajectory.

My favorite research area was probabilistic graph theory, the study of random connection of links and nodes. In fact, my PhD dissertation had been titled "On Probabilistic Graphs and Some Application." At Berkeley I was able to extend my research into areas of network reliability and vulnerability, and in 1967 I authored what would become a prize-winning paper: "Vulnerability of Communication Networks." An article I had read in the *Journal of Mathematical Biophysics* led me to a technique for analyzing random graphs. The article dealt with analyzing cell damage from radiation, but it stimulated my thinking about analyzing network damage from bombs.

As luck would have it, during my first year at Berkeley I had become friends with a fellow who was visiting the school on leave from a position at the Institute for Defense Analysis (IDA). And after my friend returned to IDA, he invited me to come to Washington to give a talk about network vulnerability. Unknown to me, one person in the audience was director of a group housed in the Office of Emergency Preparedness (OEP) in the Executive Office of the President of the United States. Months later, I received a call from this director, asking me to become a consultant. I accepted on the spot! Then, after only a couple of hours into my first consulting trip to Washington, I was invited to take a leave of absence from Berkeley and spend a year at the OEP. Again, I immediately accepted the offer.

My wife, who had just finished hanging the last set of curtains in our recently purchased new home in Walnut Creek, said she was up for the adventure. We had married during my last semester at Northwestern, and our son, five, and one-year old baby daughter, would adjust to the new environment. We would put our household in storage for a year, rent an apartment sight unseen, fly across country to a city just recovering from race riots following the assassination of Martin Luther King, and fill the apartment with rented furniture within days of arrival. Everyone at Berkeley, on the other hand, was dead-set against the idea. "You will be spoiled by the real world," the department chair told me. "The leave will change you." *I went anyway.*

I was promoted to Associate Professor while on leave. In 1969 I received the Leonard G. Abraham best paper of the year award of the IEEE Communications Society for "Vulnerability of Communication Networks." Then my one-year leave of absence stretched to two when a colleague and I decided to start a company. As a Visiting Consultant in the Office of Emergency Preparedness of the Executive Office of the President of the United States, I was in charge of a small group charged with doing something important. My group studied natural gas pipelines and built a network design system that was credited with saving over $300 million. *Business Week* published an article about our work, and newspapers around the country reported the results. This led us to form a company in 1969, the Network Analysis Corporation

(NAC). I moved to Long Island, New York, became a business executive, and never went back to Berkeley. The Berkeley prediction was correct: *I was spoiled by the real world.*

From 1969–1970 I was Executive Vice President of NAC. One year later, the company was broke, on the verge of bankruptcy, and it had a new president—me! I had no choice but to take over the helm when the original president (and my partner in the business) quit, saying he couldn't go without salary for an indefinite period. I, on the other hand, stubborn and refusing to go without a fight, asked our employees to work without regular salaries for over two years. To support my family, I borrowed tens of thousands of dollars. I ended up serving as President and Chief Executive Officer of the Network Analysis Corporation for ten years, from 1970–1980. NAC grew to become a successful telecommunications consulting and network design software firm working with major commercial and government organizations. When we outgrew the mansion in Glen Cove that served as our headquarters, we moved to a brand new office building in Great Neck.

Thanks to my background as scientific researcher, however, I did not spend the decade solely managing a growing company. I was principal investigator of NAC's contracts with the Defense Advanced Research Projects Agency of the Department of Defense. In that role, I made a number of significant contributions to the development of the ARPANet, the network that developed the technology for what eventually became the Internet. And, as NAC grew, so did my ambitions for the company. Yet, the company seemed to never have enough money or skills to become a "real player" in the Information Technology business. All this changed when I met the Vice Chairman of Continental Telephone (Contel), a $3 billion independent telephone company that was diversifying into the telecommunications field.

Contel's interest in expansion was all I needed to set NAC's wheels in motion. I created a plan—on paper—to grow NAC into a $100 million company once we were part of that much larger company, and I sold the plan to Contel! Simultaneously, I persuaded NAC's shareholders to be bought out by Contel. When Contel acquired Network

Analysis Corporation in 1980, there was dancing in the streets … but not for long. The deal called for my fellow employees and I to convert our NAC shares and stock options into a payout arrangement, the ultimate value of which would be a multiple of our 1985 earnings in the company we would build. Plus, the cost of any capital that Contel might advance us would be deducted from the payout. In effect, we were now gambling on a new venture using chips equaling our ownership of NAC and betting the whole lot on the premise that we could build a profitable business in five years.

For those five years, 1981–1985, I was President and CEO of Contel Information Systems (CIS), the systems integration subsidiary of Contel. And I worked like a dog to make CIS successful. I created CIS by merging NAC with a real-time communications software company acquired in 1981 by me with Contel's money. Like other NAC employees, I owned a minority interest in the new company. So when I sold my interest in CIS to Contel in 1985, it was for a very healthy increase over what had been paid in 1980. Soon after, I decided to leave CIS and Contel; it was time to explore other possibilities. Others, whether they stayed or left, did well also.

After leaving CIS in 1985, I decided it was time to be a consultant again. So, for a year I advised Contel on strategy, acquisitions, and mergers. I also took over the operations of a failing software and time-sharing company owned by Contel. After cutting costs, I was asked to sell the operations. So I did. I had grown far beyond my days as principal investigator, researching and solving scientific problems; the conversion to businessman was complete and irreversible.

When an executive leaves a company, he normally gets blamed for many problems in the company, even if he had not been around when the problems arose. My reputation, however, moved in the opposite direction. For example, I was credited for recommending strategies that *had* they been implemented, would have led to greater profits. As president of CIS I had proposed that Contel acquire a certain software company. We could have made the acquisition, at the time, for only $35–40 million. Contel executives declined to act on my proposal, and were astounded when that company was acquired a year later by another telephone company for $350 million. My credibility went up. My work in successfully divesting the failing software operation also was noted, because it had been losing one million dollars per month. My credibility went up. I was active in several highly visible Contel acquisitions. My credibility went up again. Two years after leaving Contel, and on the strength of my talents for strategic thinking and giving good advice, I was asked to join its board of directors—an appointment I held from 1987 until 1991, when Contel was acquired by GTE.

When I left Contel in 1985, I swore that I would never start another company. Unconvinced, my wife made me put that in writing. My oath lasted less than two years.

In 1987 opportunity beckoned, and I co-founded Network Management Inc. (NMI). For four years I served as its Chairman and Chief Executive Officer, starting with building the company by acquisition from $0 to over $50 million per year in revenues in just eighteen months. Unfortunately, the 1990 recession came along, our commercial operations suffered, and I found myself in conflict with our venture capitalist supporters. I wanted to continue to expand, while they wanted to pull back and protect their investments. We both may have been right, but I left the company in early 1991.

Tired of battling resistant Contel managers, I had operated a one-man technical and strategy consultancy, Howard Frank Associates (HFA), during the two-year hiatus between CIS and NMI. From 1985–1987 I worked with a venture capital fund and with large companies. So, after leaving NMI, I reactivated HFA, and for the next two years, 1991–1993, I served as president of Howard Frank Associates, providing business assistance and merger and acquisitions services. At the start, I was hired to find a buyer for an Atlanta based company. This turned out to be a two-year assignment that provided me with more than enough work. During the first year, I helped the company build a business strategy and a marketing plan and worked with their CFO to put their financials into a form that would survive due diligence by potential acquirers. In the second year, I developed an offering document, found a series of potential buyers, worked with management to develop presentations, and finally sold the company for a significant premium over what had been expected. During those two years I also was tapped to teach a course at the Wharton School.

Starting in 1989 and continuing until 1998, I was a senior fellow of the SEI Center for Advanced Studies in Management at the University of Pennsylvania's Wharton School. So it was not a complete surprise when, for the 1992–1993 school year, I was invited to become Adjunct Professor of Decision Sciences there, so as to develop and teach a course to MBA students titled "Science, Technology, Change, and Entrepreneurship." In 1998, I became a member of the Board of Directors of the SEI Center.

In August 1993, fortuitous events led to my appointment as Special Assistant for Information Technology Infrastructure to the Director of the Defense Advanced Research Projects Agency (DARPA). The arrangement was complex: I was on loan to the government from the University of Pennsylvania and held the position through an assignment under the Interagency Personnel Assignment Act (IPA). In 1994, I was appointed as Director of the Computing Systems Technology Office (CSTO) of DARPA after the director of that office was removed. In 1995, DARPA got a new director, who conducted a complete review of the agency. Soon after, a reorganization was announced and I was asked to become director of a combined office. I became the Director of DARPA's Information Technology Office, where I managed a $400 million annual budget aimed at advancing the frontiers of information technology.

DARPA's Information Technology Office was created to integrate all of DARPA's long-range information technology research. It contained the activities of CSTO, projects from DARPA's former Software and Intelligent Systems Office, and projects from DARPA's Defense Sciences Office. Research areas ranged from advanced microsystems and operating system design, to networking systems, to speech understanding and human–computer interaction. During my time at DARPA, I helped launch the Administration's Next Generation Internet Project as well as new programs in ultrascale computing and advanced speech understanding.

I was the founder and from 1994–1996, the first director of the DARPA/DISA Advanced Information Technology Services Joint Program Office. On the first day of my work for DAPRA, I accepted responsibility for solving a difficult technology transition problem. As part of the solution, I conceived, along with officials from the Defense Information Systems Agency (DISA), a new approach to the problem. We would create an office to facilitate the transfer of advanced technology into defense operations through DISA. It would contain DISA personnel and selected DARPA projects, all operating under DARPA's entrepreneurial policies. In effect, the office would be a "halfway house" for technology.

I also helped found and direct a joint technology office between DARPA and the National Security Administration. For the first time in a long time, the two agencies began collaborative research efforts in information technology.

At DARPA I was also co-chair and then chair of the Administration's Technology Policy Working Group, where I played a significant role in national technology policy in such areas as high definition television and adoption of commercial standards for government procurement. I was a member of the Committee on Information, Computing, and Communications of the White House's National Science and Technology Council. In recognition of my accomplishments, I was awarded the Distinguished Service Medal by the Secretary of Defense (the Defense Department's highest civilian honor) for my DARPA contributions.

My four years at DARPA were very successful. Never had I worked so hard and never had I been as influential in important areas. But the work never ended. I would be at my desk by 7:00 a.m. and stumble back home to eat dinner and then go to sleep. No one should live like this indefinitely. So I decided that I would complete my four-year appointment and return to private life. Of course, this was not the whole of it; "private life," in my case, has been somewhat of a misnomer.

Over the course of my career, I have been a member of the board of directors of several corporations, including the Analytic Services Corporation (Anser), Digex, Intek Global, Network General

Corporation, Network Management Inc., and the Contel Corporation. I have been a member of the audit, personnel, and strategy committees of many of these boards. I was a member of the Board of Directors of the Macklin Institute of Montgomery College and served on the boards of the Association for the Advancement of Collegiate Schools of Business International as well as the Mid-Atlantic Association of Colleges of Business Administration, where I was its president from 2001–2002. From 2000–2003 I was Vice Chancellor for the Americas of the International Academy of Management, a global management honorary society. I have also been a member of the AACSB Maintenance Accreditation Committee and chaired or served on the AACSB accreditation teams for a number of business schools. I was a member (2000–2005) of the Federal Advisory Committee of the National Institute of Standards and Technology's Advanced Technology Program.

I have been a member of a number of editorial boards and a featured speaker at many business and professional meetings. I co-authored three books and wrote over 190 articles in trade magazines and professional journals. I am a Fellow of the IEEE and a recipient of the IEEE's Eric Sumner award (1999), and I was elected to the National Academy of Engineering in 2002.

Whew! So about now you're asking: "how did such a tired, and definitely no longer tweedy, guy get talked into returning to academe, full-time? And what sorts of problems would be challenging enough to make him stay?

Chapter 1

In the Beginning ...

At the beginning of the fourth year of my four-year appointment at DARPA, I was contacted by a headhunter conducting a search for a dean for the business school at the University of Maryland. I knew very little about Maryland and even less about its business school. I wanted to take a year off before going back to work. So I told the headhunter that I wasn't interested. (The previous time I had been contacted about a dean's position, I had just laughed. This time I was much more polite.) However, I did say that I would be willing to send a bio in return for their written job description.

To my surprise, the description of the dean's position was interesting. It seemed they were looking for a businessman and entrepreneur who understood academia and technology, and "government experience" was a plus. On paper, I was the perfect candidate. So I agreed to an interview and entered their evaluation process.

At the start I was only mildly curious about the job. I didn't know what a dean did and what's more, wasn't sure I wanted to know. This changed during my first interview when someone asked, "What would be your strategy for the school if you were dean?" Without hesitation, I answered: "I'd make it the leading "technology-oriented" business school in the nation." The reply had just popped into my head, but as the selection process continued—and the interviewers became more forthcoming about the School's history and reputation—it became clear that such an approach was perhaps the only viable way the School could build a national and global prominence. And as soon as I spoke the words, my mild interest in the job turned to real interest.

Curiously, the strategy that seemed self-evident to me at first questioning struck my interviewers as being highly innovative and daring. Their reaction puzzled me at first; after a bit of thought I understood why my concept would appear "visionary"—if not downright alien.

Five years earlier, when I had taught that MBA course at the Wharton School—on the integration of technology and business—it evoked no interest from either the faculty or most of the Wharton students. Indeed, the Wharton administration couldn't find a single faculty member who was willing and able to teach the course, so they asked me to do it. They knew of me because a professor at Wharton (and the director of one of its research centers) was a good friend of mine. That friend had previously invited me to join the center as a senior fellow, so that I had already been traveling to Wharton two or three times a year. I had even conceived, organized, and chaired a workshop titled "The Impact of Information Technology on Business Strategy and Structure."

While my experience at Wharton taught me how little business professors (and business practitioners) knew about technology, my earlier experiences in the consulting world, on the other hand, had shown me how little technologists knew about business. Those experiences galvanized me into writing an article about the gap between business and technology, which I published in the magazine *Networking Management*. (At that point, I had been writing a management column for the magazine for about five years.)

Now, here I was, at the beginning of the interviewing process, and all of a sudden, creating a technology oriented business school sounded like a terrific idea. It would be a great project: fun and worthwhile. I now wanted the job! And I wanted it even more after spending two days at the University of Maryland being interviewed by faculty, staff, other deans, and university officials. A lunch with the deans was particularly memorable. When asked what I would do as dean, I outlined my technology vision. One dean asked, "What makes you think you can do this?"

I responded, "I haven't always had a moustache. But six months after I grew mine, moustaches started sprouting up all around my company. People follow leaders!" The questioner quickly retorted: "Lucky you didn't start wearing a brassiere!" The room exploded in laughter and when it subsided, I realized I wanted the job desperately.

Ignoring the old curse "may you get what you wish for," in September 1997 I happily became dean of the shortly-to-be-named Robert H. Smith School of Business at the University of Maryland. I had no hesitation in committing to stay dean for the five years of my initial appointment. I simultaneously was appointed professor of Management Sciences at the school, a tenured position that would be mine to claim when my service as dean ended—theoretically as soon as 2002. As dean, I would be responsible for the school's undergraduate, MBA, MS, and Ph.D. programs; the school's institutional development; and its various research and outreach centers. *So far, so good.*

Of course, and as I suspected during my brief time-outs from "*Cloud Nine*," I had a lot to learn.

When I stepped through the door to my office for the first time, in September 1997, I found myself at the helm of a "nice" but relatively unknown University of Maryland Business School. Even though it was less than twenty miles from our nation's capital, it was unable to leverage the political and international forces of the Washington DC metro area in the same way that neighboring business schools at George Washington University and Georgetown could. Worse, because the school is one part of a large, semi-autonomous College Park campus and is not located in Baltimore or another Maryland industrial center, Maryland residents did not think of it as "their" business school; consequently, it had little or no natural constituency base within the region.

The core faculty possessed respectable research reputations and teaching credentials. Its academic departments and school centers followed the hallowed academic tradition of charting their courses unfettered by managerial leadership. Faculty had the freedom to follow their own career objectives, which invariably revolved primarily around research. The school had established a solid foundation of core competencies across a range of business school offerings, including an MBA that had been transformed by the previous dean into a more "current," well-structured program. The resulting (exist-ing) curriculum was diverse and incorporated many approaches to business education, including case analyses, team problem solving, and experiential modules. However, the school had not articulated a long-range vision and was undistinguished.

In the absence of a unifying vision, the school attempted to be all things to all people: an impossible goal. Faculty and staff, over the years, had often considered potential "visions," such as becoming a school that emphasized the interaction of business and policy/regulation, or taking on an international focus, but no theme was ever compelling and powerful enough to rally the school and propel it to action. So it drifted in mediocrity.

Plus, there were other complications.

When I joined Maryland with the mission of building a technology-oriented business school, I knew nothing about the business school or being a dean. I barely knew what a dean did. I would have to be a quick study. I also discovered there had been an Acting Dean in place while the search was on; she had been not only the faculty's sole authority for a year, but a popular candidate for the dean's position. So I started the job with two short-term objectives: to stabilize the dean's office, and to learn as much as possible about the school as quickly as possible.

During the recruiting process I was unaware that the school's faculty and staff were polarized: one camp—eager to pursue fresh directions—was thrilled to see me, and wanted me to be dean; the other had supported the Acting Dean in her quest for the dean's position. She had been Associate Dean before the previous dean had left and was appointed Acting Dean until a new dean was hired. She was also empathetic, very attractive, and very smart. Half of the male faculty must have been crazy about her! My arrival brought the internal political turmoil into sharp relief, and it would not subside without intervention.

Before my arrival, the officials in the Dean's Office were the Acting Dean and an Acting Associate Dean (a professor who had temporar-ily stepped into the Associate position.) After my appointment, the

Acting Dean moved back to her Associate Dean position and the Acting Associate Dean was getting ready to return to his faculty position. I had no idea how to run a dean's office and indeed, I had no idea what the job entailed, but the one thing I did know was that I didn't want to stumble early in the job— and I was concerned that a "sour grapes" response by my newly returned to Associate Dean-ship colleague would make that stumble inevitable.

To reduce the temptation for subversion while I was finding my way, I took every opportunity to treat her well. For example, when I arrived she was occupying the Dean's Office. I told her to keep it and took an office next door. To diminish the shock of lost status, yet preserve respect for the position, I promoted her to Senior Associate Dean—so that "acting" would no longer rise to anyone's lips as a familiar part of her title—and added an Associate Dean position, to make the "acting," in that person's case, antecedent to a permanent position. I announced these promotions with fanfare, praising both individuals at every opportunity.

To my delight (and relief) the approach worked. The Dean's Office continued to function, and my Associate Dean colleagues became strong supporters. To her credit, my Senior Associate Dean functioned with dignity and enthusiasm as my deputy. Later, I was a strong advocate for her as she competed for dean of a major business school. She won the position and made a fine dean. Faculty members and administrators would over time find opportunities to confess they had not supported me for dean. To relieve their minds, I would say, "No problem. It shows that you have good taste." And when they became strong supporters, I welcomed them into the fold.

I decided to meet with every individual in the school as well as all of the other deans on the campus. And I began this project on my second day as Dean. Every day I scheduled three or four private meetings with faculty members and one or two members of the staff to gain an understanding of their individual strengths and weaknesses. I told each one at the beginning of our time together that I had three goals for the meeting: "to understand what they were doing; to learn what they thought the school needed; and to have them see me as a person rather than a name on a door."

While to me this seemed a pretty commonsense approach to finding out what people were thinking, I soon discovered it was unusual for those in academia. No other dean had ever done this, and the entire school was talking. It was only my second day, and I had already set myself up as a prime target for gossip!

As I worked through the quirky, boring, intense, distracted, charming, and ultimately incredibly diverse personalities that make up academic faculties, I learned that many in the business school were in agreement when it came to identifying our weaknesses and strengths. Almost without intent or awareness, our meetings quickly moved from "get acquainted" sessions to strategic planning sessions, often revolving around the questions: "What does it mean to be the leading technologically-oriented business school?" And, "what would such an orientation mean in terms of rankings, environment, and students?"

One professor, perceiving my motives and eager to impress, invited me to attend a meeting with her department to discuss the department's strategy. This meeting was illuminating. It showed me how non-strategic they were and how reluctant the department was to discuss its weaknesses! *But the timing was perfect.* I immediately set up similar meetings with the other academic departments (there were seven departments in all). These individual department meetings laid the groundwork for an overall strategic planning process. It took about three months on the job to get things rolling—and while the rolling was not always smooth, or in a forward direction, in that time I was able to start developing the school's first strategic plan.

Early in this process, I fearlessly articulated three specific targets for the school:

- *Ascend to the top fifteen business schools in the nation.*
- *Provide a superb research and teaching environment for faculty and students.*
- *Give our graduates a first-class ROI (return on investment) for their time and expense.*

The only way to achieve these goals, I told them, would be to build on the school's strengths, correct its weaknesses, and transform its activities and programs. Even assuming we could marshal the collective energy of the deans, chairs, and faculty once a plan was in place, the starting point—as it is in any planning process—was to take a hard look at strengths and weaknesses and develop initiatives to capitalize on the former and address the latter. With dozens of memorable individual and group meetings behind me, and yards of data files in front of me, I had no choice but be ready to take that hard look.

Strengths and Weaknesses—1997

Even though overall recognition for the School remained low, certain programs—such as the MBA program that had been ranked number twenty-five three times in the previous ten years (by *U.S. News and World Reports*), and an excellent entrepreneurship center—provided the school with a modicum of status. The school, at that time (1997) known as the Maryland Business School, had also initiated several innovative "boutique" programs, such as *Quest*, a novel undergraduate joint program between business and engineering and the College Park Scholars Initiative for superior freshmen and sophomores. Together, these programs and initiatives helped the school to garner a top twenty-five national ranking in undergraduate education (by *U.S. News and World Reports*).

In addition, while the faculty was (relatively) very small, for a public institution of the size of the University of Maryland, faculty research productivity was high. Several of our Ph.D specializations were popular with prospective students because of their program excellence. Some of the school's programmatic efforts in logistics and supply chain management and telecommunications also showed solid potential, and the school had excellent faculty in operations research. These programmatic efforts were especially important to me because they supported the technology initiative.

To our credit, the culture of the school also supported teamwork and collaboration. This strength was significant, because most schools are unable to collaborate towards overall academic goals. Those who choose to work in academia will often cite, as a primary incentive, the freedom to be left alone to pursue their own agendas. So it's rare to find an environment where faculty members can work together towards long-range school goals.

The school's strengths, as was to be expected, were offset by many weaknesses. Chief among these were inadequate resources, including too few faculty members to properly educate the volume of under-graduate students. The school had what I considered a tiny budget. How tiny? It was comparable to the round off error in my DARPA budget!

The faculty was overworked, tired, and dispirited. Professors had little self-confidence or confidence in the school's ability to become something special. There was little recognition of the school's problems or weaknesses by the university's central administration and virtually no prospect of additional university help or funding to address them. As the university's finance vice president told me, when confronted by the inequities in faculty versus student numbers, "Business schools are supposed to be milked." And he wasn't smiling when he said it. (And I wasn't smiling when I heard it!)

This sort of off-hand disclosure was unsurprising given the University's distorted view of the business school—a negativity that had helped entrench, if not exacerbate, existing weaknesses. During the summer before I became dean, I met with the outgoing "acting" provost, who was getting ready for his move, in the same position, to another university. I made detailed notes of the meeting. Among other complaints the provost felt obliged to pass along before he left were the following:

- The business school had a lack of customer orientation. We were not treating students as customers.
- The small number of freshmen that were admitted hurt campus recruiting because many potential students wanted to come to

the university to major in business but could not be admitted to our school.

• Advising was poor and focused more on processing students through the system rather than spending the time needed to give them good advice.

• Our interactions with other schools were narrow and *ad hoc* rather than showing broad thinking and long term strategic thinking.

• The business school didn't display systemic thinking (whatever that meant!).

• The business school's focus was on getting more money and not education.

Once I became dean I learned how wrong-headed these views were, but they permeated the Administration's thinking, and I continued to encounter them throughout my tenure as dean. I also realized that these views had doomed my senior associate dean's bid to become dean because these comments were also a review of her performance.

No wonder many of the faculty and staff were skeptical of their new dean and my ability to develop the school. The previous dean had also arrived with great fanfare and enthusiasm, but after several years of little progress, people had lost faith that anything would ever change.

When I say our chief weakness was that we were "under-resourced" and "under-funded" to support the volume of students that flowed into the Business School, I wasn't just drawing conclusions from anecdotes. From 1990 to 1997, school enrollments had increased by 67% compared to funding increases of only 32%. Virtually all of this growth was at the undergraduate level, where total enrollment had grown from about 2,000 to 3,500 (about 14% of the university's 24,000 undergraduate students.) To make matters worse, student class hours taught at the Business School totaled 10% of the university's total hours taught, while Business School faculty was only 5% of the comparable campus total. Four swamped advisors were advising these students. The advisors didn't have enough time to see everyone who needed help, let alone give them the individual attention they deserved. We were awash in students with too few staff, and inadequate facilities, to properly educate them all. And amazingly, no one seemed to care! (Or, perhaps more accurately, they were too busy "milking" to care). In retrospect, I suspected this was one source of the previous dean's decision to leave the university. I think he fought the battle for nearly four years and then—realizing nothing would change—simply gave up.

The existing Business School building did not have a sufficient number of classrooms to hold all of the school's classes. As a result, classes were taught in seventeen different buildings—making it impossible to build a coherent student culture. Many of these "out sourced" classrooms were run-down and technology-deficient. Most did not have computers or overhead projectors. Outside the Business School, "high tech" meant a blackboard and chalk. Because of limited funding at the outset, the Business School building had been designed and built *knowing* it would be too small to meet all of the school's needs. There were no offices available for the part-time faculty, staff members were squeezed into closet-like spaces, and there was no room for expansion. The money available to support faculty research during the summer was meager. Assistant professors would start lining up at the dean's office in October requesting funds for the following summer, but there weren't any to give them.

There is lots of data about business schools. Web sites such as those operated by *Business Week* and other magazines report numerous statistics. The individual sites of other business schools have a wealth of data about those schools and their students. I started exploring these sites, and it didn't take me more than a month to learn that faculty at business schools in the tier to which Smith aspired (like Berkeley, Michigan, or Carnegie-Mellon) carried lower teaching loads, had greater financial support for summer research, and had higher salaries.

Although the school's MBA program had been ranked twenty-fifth, none of the school's departments were ranked, and the school had the general reputation of the University of Maryland, which at that time was not even considered a top twenty public university. Because, at the time, Maryland was considered a mediocre state university, which students applied to as their "safety school," the business school was *ipso facto* thrown into the same bucket. Frankly, except for a few areas such as engineering and computer sciences, the university deserved its reputation. Recognition among business school deans, MBA directors, and corporate recruiters was low for both the undergraduate and graduate programs. This was reflected by the low score that these folks gave to the school during the annual ranking process. As a consequence, job placement opportunities for graduates did not match the caliber and potential of the best students. Starting salaries for students entering the job market were materially lower than those for students of neighboring schools such as Georgetown. Inadequate financial support for doctoral students required them to teach a number of undergraduate courses, so PhD students had less time for research. The high teaching loads affected the school's ability to attract the very best Ph.D. students. Ph.D. students at Maryland had to teach courses virtually every semester, while loads at other schools might be one or two courses during a student's final two years.

Finally, the school's alumni base (some 30,000 strong) remained virtually untapped because efforts at alumni development were primitive and under-funded. The typical response when an alumnus was contacted by a fund-raiser was: "Where have you been for the last 10 (20) (30) years?"

Count the Fingers

The Maryland business school was not just nearly unknown within Maryland, it was invisible outside of the state. To change my peers' perceptions, and at least ensure that someone out there knew I existed, I adopted a "dean of the month program." My goal was to meet at least one new dean a month—the more successful, the better. Early on, I traveled to California to meet the Stanford dean and to

New York for the dean of NYU. It turned out there were frequent deans' conferences where I could meet many at the same time, so for efficiencies' sake, I started attending those. They were eye-openers!

I remember my first deans' conference. The format for such conferences didn't change—a reception the evening before the meeting officially began, followed by one or more days' worth of sessions about managing a business school.

At the reception, deans stood around in small groups trading horror stories about mistreatment of the business school by university provosts and their difficulties with faculty. One dean declared that he never expressed an opinion in front of his provost. If he did, he said, "The provost would do exactly the opposite." Others talked about their faculty as if they were talking about raising (and disciplining!) children—children who could be, depending on the dean who was doing the talking, ungrateful, recalcitrant, willful, obstreperous, or whining.

The consensus view that provosts were a pain to be borne, if not overcome, was a real surprise; I *liked* our provost. He was honest, straightforward, and a good decision maker. Little did I know that with this provost I had drawn the equivalent of a winning mega-millions lottery ticket—and that after he left to become president of a midwestern university, this nearly unique set of qualities would be lost, never to be seen again in any subsequent provost. As to the child-like qualities of academics, having been a faculty member at the beginning of my career and also having many professors as friends, I had not yet developed a jaundiced view of them. I liked them, thought I was capable of dealing with them as colleagues, and was taken aback by the deans' views.

One battle-hardened dean asked me: "What's the real job of a dean?" Since I didn't have the answer, he gave it to me: "To keep the 50% of the faculty who hate you away from the 50% who haven't made up their minds." I chuckled good naturedly, but the dean was not finished: "How do you know which 50% hate you?" Again, he gave me the answer: "At the end of the day, you walk in the parking lot and when you see a faculty member, wave. Then count the number of fingers that he waves back."

I learned an astounding fact: The average tenure of a dean at a business school was about four years. That was not just how long they lasted at *bad* schools, it was how long they could stand the job, on average, at *all* schools. Deans talked freely about the life cycle of a dean's attitude towards the university and the job—how they started with enthusiasm, then moved to disillusionment, despondence, and ultimately, dislike. I was also given a *Fortune* article, "What's Killing the Business Deans of America (August 1992). According to the article, "... august business schools are nearly impossible to manage. Strange cultures, bizarre organizational structures and weird attempts at democracy make them messier than all but the looniest for-profit company." The article's answer to what's killing the deans? It was faculty and alumni.

There I was, barely into my first five years of employment, and people out there were already predicting my early demise. I guess they didn't know how well my past had prepared me for "strange cultures, bizarre organizational structures and weird attempts at democracy."

Chapter 2

Then There's a Plan

The school's first strategic plan, adopted in January 1998, proposed a dual strategy to build distinction: develop first rate academic areas and centers with distinguished research, teaching, and outreach; and differentiate our school with around creation, management, and deployment of knowledge and information.

Implementing these strategies required acceptance by a large portion of faculty members, including the majority who had not yet bought into technology-differentiation. After all, technology differentiation without excellence in core business school functions could lead to mediocre business programs, while improving core functions without establishing technological differentiation would keep us marching in place, business as usual. It was clear that we had to do two things simultaneously: build the overall quality of the faculty and increase its technology competencies. This would be no mean feat, but it had to be done. Since only about a third of the faculty believed in the technology differentiation strategy, it was vital to continue to build core business strengths in conventional areas such as finance, marketing, and management. Without such efforts, the unbelievers would have revolted (via passive resistance) and the technology strategy would have failed.

After discussion, six key strategic goals emerged from the plan:

1. To enhance research excellence,
2. To create academic program distinctions,
3. To extend the cross-functional linkages within the school and across the university,
4. To advance information technology as a core competency,

5. To market the distinctions of the school,

6. To improve the school's resources and infrastructure.

The strategic plan delineated specific targeted activities designed to move the school forward towards achieving these six goals. The parties responsible for their implementation were identified. In some cases, individuals carried out the implementation, but in others, groups of department chairs and members of the dean's office were assigned tasks. Here was where the special collaborative nature of the faculty came into play. Without it, I wouldn't have been able to get people focused and cooperating in implementing the plan.

We would have to create a new business school model around the creation, management, and deployment of knowledge and information. Content innovations in the curriculum would be required. A new series of MBA concentrations: telecommunications, technology management, electronic commerce, financial engineering, and supply chain and logistics management were part of the new model. These would be rolled out over the next eighteen months.

We didn't have the faculty to create either research excellence or academic program distinctions. Therefore, we would have to hire and retain a number of top tenure-track faculty. Unfortunately, the school had no money to hire faculty and the university would not give the school a dime to do so. Therefore, generating revenues to pay for new faculty became a high priority.

Similarly, our faculty was overloaded. To enhance their research productivity and give them time to work on new programs, the school had to reduce their teaching burden. To do so would lead us to use some very non-traditional hiring approaches.

Improving the future of our students was also part of the plan. Strengthening undergraduate and MBA job placement statistics was one step. An organized campaign to attract corporate recruiters and programs to enhance career mentoring for both graduate and undergraduate students would be needed.

Additionally, the strategic plan recognized the need to increase financial support for top quality Masters and Ph.D. students and improve national program rankings through placement and student career skills advances, strategic marketing, and leadership in curriculum innovation.

Finally, the school needed to increase its external visibility in academic and corporate circles. It would do this by building a strategic marketing program centered on the technology-differentiation strategy.

Naming the School

Getting the school moving would be a monumental task. Like in any academic institution, challenging the status quo was not for the timid. Each department and business unit, and the school as a whole, would have to undertake activities that spanned all phases of the school's operations. Each of the initiatives would impact the school's ability to generate revenue; student enrollment; program development; faculty hiring, salaries, and retention; marketing strategies; facilities; and the need to mobilize alumni. We would have to change in spite of the university's inertia and academia's natural hostility towards change.

Our initial momentum came from the announcement of a $15 million naming gift for the school in April 1998. The school would formally become the Robert H. Smith School of Business.

The naming of the school was a major event. I had met Robert H. Smith during my first semester as dean when he had come to the school to give a talk to our MBA students. He must have enjoyed himself, because early in 1998 in a private discussion with the university's president, he expressed interest in naming the school. He requested a plan for what we would do to become a top-fifteen business school. I found out about this interest when the president asked to see me late on a Friday. Since I hadn't done much of anything yet, I had no idea of the purpose of the meeting. When I met with him, he told me about a "possible donor" who might like to name the school. The president asked me to develop a "top-fifteen" plan for the donor. My response was: "I already have one. I will send it to you on Monday."

I sent the president a fifteen-page plan. His direction was to shorten it to about four pages and remove the section on weaknesses. I did shorten it but refused to eliminate discussion of weaknesses because I believed that without addressing weaknesses, a strategic plan was nothing more than a fantasy. I debated with him, and he agreed to include the following paragraph in our four-page "Vision":

> There are barriers to achieving the vision and, unless re- moved, they hamper our ability to move forward. We are at a disadvantage in competing for outstanding new faculty hires with the top schools because of too few distinguished endowed chairs and research professorships. A central determinant of rankings in *US News* is placement indica- tors. However, our MBA and undergraduate placement measures do not match the caliber of the student body. We will need specific, targeted efforts to improve these indica- tors. The external community's general impression of the Maryland Business School (referring here to both academic and corporate observers) under-represents true program quality. The school must increase its promotional activities to achieve the recognition that it currently deserves and to then raise the level of its recognition to the level that the school will achieve in the next five years. Space limita- tions in our current facilities hinder growth opportunities. Van Munching Hall is a first class facility but does not have sufficient classroom or office space and will be unable to accommodate the growth required for the next stage in the school's development.

The president called another meeting. Attending were the provost, the university's vice president of finance, and me. The president told us that the donor wanted to know what we would do about our space problems, since the plan indicated that without more space, we could not grow. We quickly found an answer: We would build a 6,000 sq. ft. addition to the business school's building at $200 per square foot. We would use $3 million of the naming gift, the university would contribute $3 million, and we would borrow $6 million to finance the building. The four of us wrote and signed a Memorandum of Agreement, and I walked out with a deal to build an addition to the school. This was an amazing accomplishment in its own right because there had not been any plan to expand our facilities and the prospects of getting such an agreement had seemed to be virtually zero. I was elated—literally jumping up and down with joy.

Several weeks later, we met with Bob Smith. He had made numerous notes on the document and questioned me for an hour. At the end of the meeting the president and provost congratulated me for the way I had handled the questions. A month later, Bob Smith called the president and told him we had a deal. The school would become the "Robert H. Smith School of Business." The naming gift agreement required the university to support the expansion of the school's physical facility, Van Munching Hall. This required approval by the Board of Regents and was approved without delay. So, six months after becoming dean, the school had a new name, we would be receiving $15 million, and we had a plan to expand Van Munching Hall, something that had not been in the university's long-range campus facility plan.

12,000 Becomes 103,000

Naming the school and having an approved building expansion was a great start. It made me a hero with the faculty, many of whom had been in a "wait and see" mode. Bob Smith, a brilliant entrepreneurial businessman, proposed a terrific following act. The naming of the school had not yet been announced. Bob suggested that the president go to the Governor of Maryland with a proposition: "If the Governor would provide $6 million for the business school building, the president could bring in a $15 million contribution for the naming of the school." Amazingly, the Governor agreed! (The fact that this was an election year probably contributed to his agreement.)

In the original response to Bob Smith's question, the university had been coerced into agreeing to contribute $3 million for the building. Now, with the State's $6 million, they stated to me that I didn't need their money. To counter this point, I began a campaign of lobbying the provost, the president, and the chief financial officer to retain the university's $3 million. Each time I saw any of them, I would bring the topic up.

My argument was simple and irrefutable. The campus was short of classrooms. Adding classrooms in Van Munching Hall was as good as adding classrooms anywhere else on campus because our use of classrooms elsewhere on campus would be reduced. With the State's and campus dollars, we could build a larger building. We could use the State's $6 million, the university's $3 million, and a borrowed $9 million to build an $18 million, 9,000 sq. ft. building. After months of pestering, the university agreed.

A larger building would be useful, but a 9,000 sq. ft. facility would still be too small. I began asking (politely) the question: "If I had $6 million cash to add to the $18 million, could I build a $24 million building?" The answer from everyone was "if you have the need and the cash, you can build it larger." So I began talking about the project as "a $24 million" project. We didn't have the cash, but no one corrected me.

We began preliminary work on a $24 million plan and also began looking for a $6 million naming gift for the Van Munching Hall "Annex." Magic followed. I went off to London with my wife for a short vacation. When I returned, my senior associate dean reported that Leo Van Munching, a 1950 graduate of the school and the donor who had supported the original building construction had called her and offered to donate $6 million for the Annex. Wow!! We had a $24 million project!

But it would still not be big enough to meet all of our requirements. So I asked another question: "If I could show how we would pay a $15 million loan, could we expand the project again and build a $30 million building?"

And the process continued. In the end, we built a 103,000 sq. ft building costing $43 million. The project took three years from concept to occupancy. It was the fastest significant building erected on campus. (The original Van Munching Hall took 15 years from initial plan to move-in.)

The Undergraduate Problem

The result of expanding the undergraduate body over the last seven years (from about 2,000 to over 3,500) had been to yield a mediocre group of students, many of whom had no chance of graduating. I began to understand this problem about a year after becoming dean.

In my first year as dean I had no sense of the dimensions of the undergraduate problem. A weak assistant dean was responsible for undergraduates. There didn't seem to be much interest in undergraduates. This changed after I fired the assistant dean and hired a dynamo who quickly identified the problem and the university's unwillingness to deal with it.

When told of the situation, I was dismayed that neither the university administration nor the previous business school administration had done anything about the issue. The university had no interest in it, and the previous dean had complained vociferously but had gotten nowhere. When my new assistant dean told me that "nothing could be done," my response was that "There is always something that can be done. For example, we could change the grading of the core courses and flunk out half the students. All I have to do is talk to a few faculty members teaching the lower level courses to make this happen." I then added, "You don't know me or whether I would do this. So why don't you tell people that I am whispering that I might do this."

Then, in my usual monthly meeting with the university's provost, I repeated what I had said and added: "I'd rather not do this but I might be forced to."

We began working with the provost on a new undergraduate admissions policy.

Merging Two Departments—the Corporate Way

The business school had seven academic departments, including a mature Management Sciences and Statistics Department (MSS) with about a dozen faculty and a young Information Systems Department (IS) with six faculty (one full professor, one associate professor, and four junior faculty.) During my first strategic reviews, I concluded that the Management Sciences department was top heavy, conservative, and had limited prospects for growth. Ironically, I myself had my academic appointment in this department.

The IS group was too small; its faculty was overworked and approaching burnout. The junior faculty were being abused by having to do too much teaching and work on service projects. The field had great growth prospects, but the department had little chance to grow because it was below critical mass. It was obvious to my senior associate dean and me that the two groups needed to merge. Getting this to happen would be another story.

Change in academia is difficult. The normal way to explore a department merger is to appoint a committee of faculty from both departments, have them study the problem for a year, and then report their conclusions. By the end, everyone would hate everyone else, and there would be numerous reasons why a merger was a bad idea. If a merger did take place, it would be sure to fail.

I decided to do it the corporate way. We met, on a Thursday, with two senior professors from the MSS department whom we had chosen to lead the combined operation. They agreed to take over the merged operation and were sworn to secrecy. On Monday, I met with the chair of the IS department and bought her acquiescence with a deal she couldn't refuse. I announced the merger on Wednesday, effective Thursday morning.

Thursday afternoon, I met with the faculties of the new department, discussed strategy, and assigned responsibilities including picking a name for the new department. The name selected was "Decision and Information Systems." I also made a prediction: "In five years, the new department will double in size and become one of the best such departments in the world." My prediction was correct.

The new department, today called Decision, Operations, and Information Technologies, is the school's largest department, with about thirty-five faculty members. The department contains key behaviorial, information technology, computer sciences, telecommunications, and operations research and statistics capabilities. This department has established itself as a leader in both information systems and operations research, with the research of both groups of faculty being ranked at the very top of the profession.

My corporate-style reorganization had unexpected ramifications. When my senior associate dean was meeting faculty at another business school, she was questioned about the merger. Her strong support of me led to her rejection as that school's next dean. Also, the former chair of the IS department moved on to another school, the associate professor left, and the assistant professors are no longer with the school. Nonetheless, many great IS faculty joined the school, and IS research at Smith is consistently rated in the top three in the country.

A New Admissions Policy

In theory the existing undergraduate admissions policy was reasonable. Students were admitted to the business school in the second semester of their sophomore year. Acceptance required a 2.8 grade point average and successful completion of the business core: two accounting courses, a business statistics course, an economics course, and calculus.

As an admissions attraction, the university told potential students that they had "provisional admittance" to the business school when entering the university as freshmen. They were told that they would have to meet the admission requirements for the provisional label to be removed. But no one did anything about the students who didn't meet requirements.

Many unqualified students were admitted, and the school had hundreds of students who thought they were business students but who would never graduate with business degrees. Indeed, many of these students would never graduate with any degree.

No one had the will to tell these students that they weren't in the business school. The university refused to enforce the admissions policy. Business school staff didn't have the capacity or the direction to take on the monumental task of throwing out hundreds of students.

I, with the support of my new Assistant Dean for Undergraduate Studies, was ready to take on the challenge. But, for a long-term solution, we needed a better admissions policy with a higher required GPA and with no provisional students.

After much debate spanning more than a year, the provost consented to a new admissions policy. We would require a minimum 3.0 GPA for admittance to the business school as a junior. We would eliminate provisional admits but instead admit up to 400 highly qualified freshmen directly into the school. These would be called "Direct Admits" and would need at least a 1300 (out of 1600) score on the SAT. We agreed to cap the junior class at 800 students. That is, we would admit enough students each year so that the direct admits and the junior admits would total 800. (Because we had many more students, it would take years to reach this goal.) We agreed to a sliding GPA for junior admission so that we would always be able to meet the 800-student goal. Therefore, the required 3.0 GPA might go up or down in a given year depending on the number of students applying to the school.

The total number of students slowly declined with the new admission policy. It would take about five years to reach the 800-student cap, but by the time we did, we had a spectacular undergraduate student body.

Even though we agreed reluctantly to the risk of the Direct Admit policy, it turned out to be one of my best decisions. The first year, we had 137 direct admits with SATs of 1365, compared to university freshmen, who had average SATs of about 900. The second year we had about 250 direct admits, and by the fifth year, we were enrolling about 400 students with SATs of 1360 and high school GPAs of 3.9. We would get over 4,000 applications for the 400 slots. These students turned out to have the highest retention and graduation rates on campus.

The policy on junior admits turned out to be equally effective. The number of juniors in the school slowly declined towards our 800-student goal. It now took about a 3.5 GPA in the first two years at Maryland to get into the business school as a junior.

Our students were wonderful. We loved them and they loved the school, but no one outside the business school loved us. Deans of other colleges who had to take our rejected students resented us. Students who didn't make it into Smith disliked us. They were also jealous of our superior facilities because there were many poor buildings on campus. Campus administrators who had approved the admissions policy searched for ways to subvert it and to accept students who didn't meet the requirements.

Our campus was a socialistic environment where many believed that any student wanting to become a business student should be admitted to Smith. The staff hated us because we were throwing students out of the school when they didn't make the grade. It takes a lot of work to reject a student because his or her entire academic record must be reviewed before it can be done. We threw out hundreds.

Students have parents, and parents can be counted on to complain when their children are demoted. Without fail, the president's and provost's offices would get irate telephone calls from parents. This meant more work for the staff members who had to field the calls. They had to review the files as well as all correspondence and warnings to the student, write letters to parents, and be lambasted by them in phone calls. Lawsuits were frequently threatened, so this meant even more work.

I would get an occasional call. One such call from an angry father went like this: (I am paraphrasing) "You have expelled my son from the business school. You need to readmit him. It's not his fault that he was drunk all of last year and failed his courses. The university should have kept him sober."

I argued with the father for about ten minutes and then realized that the call was going nowhere so concluded it by saying: "Sir, we can spend another hour on this call, another ten minutes, or another minute. At the end of this time, you son will still not be in the business school." The father said "Thank you," and hung up.

We persevered. Continuous vigilance was our byword. If we let anything get by, they would do it to us again. Throughout all this, my assistant dean was a stalwart. I couldn't have done it alone, but with her, we transformed the undergraduate student body from mediocre to one of the best in the country. The transformation included many elements:

- Improving the physical infrastructure and teaching environment
- Dealing with the teaching load problem
- Enhancing courses
- Creating niche programs
- Improving teaching quality and full-time faculty coverage

Faculty Hiring and Salaries

I announced a three-year program to bring faculty salaries to parity with aspirational peers. Its goal: the top 25% of the faculty would be paid at the 75th percentile of the target schools (defined as the ten US schools paying the highest salaries). In the first year of the program, salary increases averaged 10%, with more than twenty faculty members receiving raises of 14.9%. (The president had to approve any raise of 15% or higher.)

At that time I had no idea that there were salary raise pool constraints and therefore didn't know that I had violated them. Somehow, the provost found a way to fix this problem. Salary increases were based on academic performance rather than longevity or whether or not particular faculty members endorsed the technology differentiation direction the school had taken.

Four years after its initiation, faculty salaries matched those of faculty at the top ten business schools at both the 50th and 75th percentiles. Note that comparing averages among different schools can be risky because faculty salaries vary considerably across disciplines and the exact functional composition of each rank can significantly affect the school-wide average salary. (For example, faculty salaries in finance are much higher than salaries in human resources, so if a school has more finance people, its salaries will be higher.)

The school developed a long-range hiring plan aimed at expanding the number of top faculty in each department. Targeted hires accelerated the school's progress in shifting to a technology focus and helped it implement initiatives that would bring distinction to the school. We began by searching for an endowed chair in information systems using some of Bob Smith's endowment. We were able to attract a terrific individual who had been a full professor and former chair of the IS department at NYU.

Pepsico donated $1 million to the school. We used the money to create a Pepsico Chair in Marketing. It took a year to fill the position, but we were able to hire a great marketing expert. Another top marketing scholar visited the school to give a guest lecture. We were able to lure him away from Vanderbilt to become our next chair of the marketing department and also an endowed Smith chair.

The dean plays a major role in recruiting leading academics. I was no exception. I would meet with candidates and describe our vision and strategy. Over lunches and dinners I would learn what they needed to come to Maryland. Often this was more than money. It could involve additional hires and resources in their areas. Where it made sense to me, I made the commitments. When recruiting a top professor, there can be many false alarms. You may go through all the motions, make a salary offer, and negotiate an agreement. At the last minute, the professor's institution may choose to match the offer. The only winner in this transaction is the professor who stays at his original school with a much higher salary.

While we were attempting to recruit stars from other universities, other universities were trying to recruit our stars. We had the money and the endowed positions to retain some of our best scholars. We did so when they came to me with competing offers. When they had excellent offers from fine institutions, I matched them. To do this, I would have to write a justification for the raise for approval by the president. If their offers were from mediocre places, I wished them good luck and "bon voyage." In this way, we prevented a number of fine researchers and teachers from moving to other universities.

One year we were able to attract world-renowned scholars in finance from Duke and in marketing from Michigan. Smith was on the move.

We had a detailed five-year hiring plan that identified future hires by department and scholarship area. In some years we hired more than our projected number of professors because more excellent candidates were available than expected. We would compensate by not hiring in a future year. In other years, a department might skip hiring because we couldn't attract a top scholar. We would roll over the hire to the following year. Initially, departments were reluctant to skip hiring in a year because they feared that the open positions would be taken away from them. After a couple of years, the departments developed confidence that I would not take back open positions. The approach helped build an "only the best" attitude at the school.

Over a ten-year period, approximately one hundred new faculty members joined the school. In the same period, some faculty retired and some moved to other places. In all, the school faculty grew from about seventy to over 150. This expansion of school faculty represents one of the most successful business-school recruiting programs ever. The quality of this new pool was extraordinary. By the end of my term, 38% of our full professors had endowed positions. During my tenure, the *Financial Times* ranked the school in the top ten in research in the world (as measured by the number of papers published in top business journals), and the *Business Week* rankings placed faculty intellectual contributions at number three.

A final strategic move came with the creation of a new faculty category. A limited number of non-tenure track, permanent, "superstar," teaching faculty were hired to address teaching needs across all programs. These teachers, originally termed "teaching professors," held terminal degrees (Ph.D.s and the like) and possessed outstanding teaching skills. Since no research was expected, teaching professors carried heavier course loads than tenure-track faculty and assisted in various service and student support activities. Teaching professors held three-year renewable contracts and were part of the life of the school. As such, they managed programs, advised students, and contributed to the general well being of the school. The quality of teaching in the undergraduate program improved, and the teaching burden of the tenure-track faculty was reduced.

When I stepped down as dean, more than 175 faculty worked in the school. This included over one hundred tenure-track professors, twenty teaching professors, about a dozen visitors and full-time lecturers, and a variety of adjuncts and Ph.D. student graduate assistants.

My First Crisis

I received a call from the provost's office. Someone had sent an anonymous letter to several deans on campus charging that the business school was sending inflated data to US News and World Reports for use in their annual MBA rankings. The letter stated that the school was covering this up and that the practice had been going on for years.

My initial reaction was alarm because I really didn't know if the allegations were true. Upon investigation, I learned that a business school faculty member had made similar charges several years before. The school had appointed two committees to look into the charges. One, headed by the chair of the Accounting Department, had audited the school's data submissions. The audit had found that the school's data were accurate and that there was no misrepresentation. The committees reported their findings to the school at a monthly school assembly. Apparently, whoever had written the letter was not convinced or wanted to damage the school no matter what was the truth. (Or both!)

Responding to an anonymous letter can be a no win situation. More people learn about the charges and the response can lend credibility to the original charges. Nonetheless, I decided that I couldn't leave the charges unanswered and wrote a letter to every dean on campus, summarizing the charges and answering them point-by-point. In response, I received nice notes from deans, and the problem seemed to be resolved.

Several months later, my senior associate dean received a call from a business school dean at another university. That dean had received an anonymous letter repeating the same charges and quoting the Maryland letter. He faxed us the letter. We couldn't tell whether this was the same or a different letter writer since there were many people on campus who disliked the business school. We didn't know who else had received the letter.

We again debated the virtues of answering the charges or ignoring them. I decided that I couldn't be silent, so I crafted a letter answering the charges. I also summarized all of the good things that were happening at Maryland and attached a copy of our submission to *US News and World Reports* to show what we had submitted. I sent this to every dean at every business school in America.

The response was heartening. E-mails of support flooded in. Many deans shared that they too had been victims of anonymous charges. Many of the responses were "When I get an anonymous letter, I throw it away."

Our school's reaction was also positive. People closed ranks and united in support of the school and me. I was asked in public "How do we get the bastard?" My response: "It's not fruitful to conduct a witch hunt. We need to move forward."

The ultimate accolade came at a business school deans' meeting a few months latter. One dean approached me: "We've been watching your progress at Maryland," he said. "We'd like to invite you to join the Board of Directors of the AACSB." The AACSB is the organization that accredits business schools. Naturally, I accepted.

The Strategic Planning Process

Our early rudimentary efforts at strategic planning became more sophisticated. The school now operated under a continuous improvement model spearheaded by its strategic planning process. Under this model, annual and five-year objectives and tactics were set in six areas: Research, academic programs, the Smith Community, Information Technology, Marketing, and Resources and Infrastructure.

Each department (academic and staff) participated in the strategic plan, set strategic objectives for itself, and collaborated in the statement of objectives for the school. The school's department chairs and senior staff (assistant deans, associate deans, and department directors), led by the dean's office, insured the implementation of the objectives.

The strategic planning process operated on the following timetable:

- June – Finalize Faculty Recruiting Plan
- September – Satisfaction Surveys Completed for Baseline
  - Faculty Satisfaction
  - Undergraduate Student Satisfaction
  - MBA Student Satisfaction
  - External Rankings
- November – Management Strategy Retreat
- February – Present Department Strategic Plans and Research Metrics
- March–April – Integration of Strategies, Plans, and Financial Forecasts
- May – Strategic Plan Presented at School Assembly and to MBA Students
- May – Draft Plan Published for Review and Feedback
- April–May – Strategic Personnel Objectives for Next Year
- June – Plan Published
- August – The Strategy Process Begins Again

The key elements for the success of the plan were the following:

- The Mission and Vision had to be robust, meaningful, and inclusive and communicated frequently.
- Strengths, weaknesses, and challenges needed to be real and perceived as honest.
- The plan had to strive to differentiate the school from its competition.
- The strategic planning process needed to be structured and inclusive. All parties needed to be involved.
- Financial realities and resources needed to be part of the plan.
- There couldn't be a "them and us" mentality or a "parent/child" relationship between the dean's office and the faculty. Collaboration was essential.
- It wasn't necessary to convince everyone, but there had to be a "get on the train or be left behind" atmosphere.
- The dean needed to be the leader and the cheerleader.
- The process had to be continuous, with realistic milestones and frequent feedback on accomplishments with measurable milestones and real metrics.
- The plan had to be framed in terms of incremental annual progress but transformational long term progress.
- New sources of revenue and new models of revenue generation were required.
- The school could either move up or down—maintaining the *status quo* was not likely.

As part of the planning process, we commissioned several satisfaction surveys covering students, staff, faculty, and alumni. Some surveys were conducted by an organization affiliated with the AACSB and compared the business school to peers and the overall population of business schools who had undertaken the surveys. Therefore, we were able to view the school's performance within a group of seven schools and across the larger population. Other data came from business school rankings and business school websites. Here is an example from our faculty survey:

1998 AACSB Management
Education Faculty Satisfaction Survey

Seven Designated Schools: U Maryland, Penn State, U of Washington, Indiana U, U of Minnesota, Vanderbilt U, U North Carolina, plus others for a total of seventy-one schools. The messages from the survey were clear. We needed to improve support, teaching loads, and teaching quality, and we needed to lower class sizes. In subsequent years, we would improve performance on each of these measures.

University of Maryland	Rank Among 7 Schools	Rank All 71 Schools
Areas of Least Satisfaction		
Level of support for secretarial assistance	6	64
Quality of teaching in UG courses	6	62
Average class size	6	54
Level of support for international activities	6	49
Amount of exposure for specific discipline in UG program	6	46
Quality of students in UG program	6	46
Teaching load	6	44
Placement services for students	6	28
Amount of exposure for specific discipline in MBA program	6	25
Recruiting of quality students for the doctoral program	6	16
Level of faculty development support to enhance computer apps to support teaching	5	49
Level of support for professional service	5	46
Level of support for school service	5	46
Level of faculty development support to enhance awareness of new technology	5	44
Level of support for travel	5	41
Level of support for computer hardware technology	5	38
Quality of design of the UG curricula	5	34
Level of support for research grants	5	34
Quality of teaching in required courses for MBA program	5	25
Doctoral program preparation for teaching	5	11

Chapter 3

Struggles to Keep to the Plan

Turning Faculty into Entrepreneurs

O ne thing was sure. The university would not give us any money. They did, however agree to allow us to keep a significant part of any additional revenues we could generate by ourselves. No one, including me, realized how significant these revenues would become, but by the time the administration did, we had had incredible growth.

So a new task for me was to turn the school from a typical academic institution into an entrepreneurial powerhouse. A key to this was to show the faculty how they would benefit from additional revenues. Nearly all academics are financially conservative and risk adverse. Even business professors are unlikely to have ever run a business, and few are interested in this endeavor. What's more, the relationship between a dean and his or her faculty is usually like a typical parent and child. The child goes to the parent and asks for something. The parent says, "No, we can't afford it." The child says, "but I want it" and leaves the dean's office upset or angry.

When I became dean, I discovered that there was no formal budget for the school, and therefore monthly reports of "actual versus budget" didn't exist. This was a source of considerable frustration. I first tried to train the financial staff to produce these reports but discovered that both the staff and the university's financial reporting were incompetent.

Every one else in the school was also in the dark. So, when the dean said, "we can't afford it," the statement had little credibility. The faculty and staff thought that the school was rich while the reality was that the school was poor. But no one knew this.

To try to understand what was going on, I began building a spreadsheet of the school's revenues and costs. It took months to get to a reasonable model because there was no baseline to go by. When it was reasonably complete, I decided to present the results to the faculty in the school's monthly faculty/staff assembly. This was a huge change from earlier deans who were said to "manage from their hip-pockets." That is, when asked for money for a new project, earlier deans would pretend to look in their pockets and respond with "I have no money."

Every assembly began with a report from the dean about the school's progress. I started including a report on the school's finances. Then, when asked by a faculty member for money for a new project, I would open up the financial model (which was on my desktop PC) and tell the supplicant: "We have two ways to fund it. Either generate more revenues or cut something. What would you like to cut?" Since no one wanted to cut anything (in reality there was nothing to cut), the requestor would walk out of my office with the sense that we needed to generate more revenue.

We began looking for ways to build revenues. One thought was to start part-time MBA programs in different locations around the region. We hired a consultant to study nearby markets for MBA demand. The study identified Baltimore and Washington as likely targets. We selected Baltimore, Maryland to be the location of the first such venture. This was as much a political decision as a market one because it would have been difficult to get approval from the administration for an out of state venture before going to Baltimore.

Any new venture would have to be proposed to the faculty for a vote to proceed. Our faculty was overworked and overloaded and unlikely to vote for anything that increased their workload. I decided to follow a multi-step process for approval. First, instead of requesting approval, I made a presentation at the assembly about the school's strategic plan, including a five-year financial forecast and a forecast of how increases in revenues would be spent. This was a radical departure from past norms.

Include in the presentation was a detailed table showing how an additional $1 million would be spent. Here is the table:

What $1 Million Will Buy		
Use	Expenditure	Impact
3 Tenure Track Faculty	$375 K	Lower Loads, Greater Depth
1 Non Tenure Track	60	Lower Loads
Faculty Retention	100	Salary Competitiveness
Summer Research Funds	100	Increase Research
Information Technology	100	Improve Productivity
Graduate Student Support	40	Superior Students
Career Services Support	25	Higher Starting Salaries, Rankings
Strategic Marketing	50	Increased Rankings
Revenue Generating Invest	100	Future Revenue Increases
G&A/Contingency	50	Greater Responsiveness

For the first time, faculty could relate growth in revenues to their own self-interest. They could see that they would be the direct beneficiaries of the increased dollars.

A month later I returned to the faculty assembly, made a detailed presentation about a possible expansion to Baltimore, showed the $1 million slide again, and requested a vote to proceed. The vote was unanimously in favor.

Continued Expansion

We launched the Baltimore operation during the next academic year. It was successful, the $1 million of increased revenues materialized, and we spent the proceeds in line with the plan. Given this success, we had no problem getting agreement to expand to other locations. Further, we would generate additional revenues by "market pricing" MBA tuition. We started a part-time evening program in Washington, DC, and the following year, we started a weekend program in

Washington. We had done detailed market research before starting the evening Washington program. The response was so good that I unilaterally decide to launch the weekend program. It too was a resounding success.

As part of the expansion program, the school, with the agreement of the university, developed a "differential tuition" plan where MBA tuition was priced at the market rate rather than at the lower rates charged for the University of Maryland's general graduate programs. The school retained 75% of the incremental tuition generated for its College Park based, full-time MBA program and all of the revenues generated off campus.

When we negotiated this agreement, off campus revenues came from a small, low cost program in Shady Grove, Maryland. We had not yet thought about expansion to other locations and consequently, the university did not pay much attention to this financial element of our plan because our forecast for these revenues was small. However, because of Maryland's public university tuition, the program was the lowest cost part-time MBA program in the region—indeed, it was underpriced for what was being offered.

With university approval, we increased off campus tuition by 60% for new students and embarked on a strategy of increasing off campus tuition and fees by 10% per year for the foreseeable future. Not surprisingly, applications increased and the quality of these applications also increased. Revenues rolled in.

From about two hundred students in 1999, the student population expanded to over 1,000 within ten years. Revenues increased from about $1 million to more than $15 million. This rapid revenue growth awoke the greed of the university's central administration. Simply put, they wanted a piece of the action.

Fighting to Keep Our Revenues

The Smith School had become a capitalistic enterprise within a socialistic system. The business school was going from a poverty stricken small school to a self-sustaining wealthy empire. Outside of the school, other deans, faculty, and administrators were jealous. The university's administration began looking for ways to get some of our money either by cutting our budget or increasing our taxes.

Some of the budget cuts were small, such as when the school's access funds (a mere $90,000 per year) for subsidizing courses taught by business faculty to non-business school students were reduced by two thirds. I responded by cutting the most important non-business school courses. After taking these actions I received a telephone call from the university's dean of Undergraduate Studies. "You can't do this," she told me. "I already have," I responded. "Well, I am going to tell the provost." "You do that," I said. Two weeks later, I had our money back.

Another series of cuts that still anger me were more significant. During a series of recession years, the State of Maryland's contributions to the University of Maryland were reduced. The university's response was to take back money from its units. But instead of cutting our state subsidy (about 40% of our total), the university took its cut on our total revenues. This cost us 2.5 times as much as it cost the other schools because they didn't have externally generated revenues. I complained vigorously but couldn't get any relief from the cuts. The answer was always the same: "We applied the same cuts to everyone and everyone was treated the same."

The university was accustomed to passive acceptance of its actions. I decided that I couldn't let this take place. I had no power to reverse the cuts, but I pointed out to our department chairs and managers: "If I don't do something significant, they will think that they can do it again." So, I cancelled the most visible program being offered to non-business students (an entrepreneurship "citation"). Years later, this action would still be thrown at me as an example of why I was not a good "campus citizen."

It would take a separate book to document the small cuts, the broken promises, and the ways that the university violated its basic premise of equity to all. But through it all, we found ways to continue expanding, adding new revenue sources, building our school, and growing beyond the constraints of a "state" school. Ten years later, our revenues had grown more than fourfold and the school was basically financially independent of its university parent. We were the only school on campus that was sending more money to the university than we were receiving in state subsidy from the university.

Borrowing from the University

The university's support of the business school was not totally absent. Starting from a near poverty level, we had no capital to invest in expansion. The university loaned us (with interest) $750,000 to hire faculty and to build facilities in Washington, DC. to support our Washington part-time MBA program expansion.

When I discovered that we were $1 million in deficit because of the earlier "advances" from the Foundation, I had no way of making this up in a single year. I decided to ignore the problem because it was not of my making. To do otherwise would have forced me to cut programs and expenses and would have stopped our expansion in its tracks.

As part of my effort to find money, I observed that the university was booking summer school tuitions in the year following the summer that the courses were taught. However, about half of these courses were being taught in the preceding fiscal year because the new fiscal year started on July 1 and we taught courses in June. According to accepted accounting procedures, these revenues should have been booked in the previous year. This would yield a $600,000 revenue windfall for the business school. I discussed the opportunity with the university's controller and came to an agreement that we could book the revenues.

Believing that we had an extra $600,000 to spend, we spent it. Unfortunately, the university's chief financial officer reversed the controller's decision at the end of the year so that I was another $600,000 in the hole. (About three years later, the university must have learned that position was incorrect because they changed their revenue recognition policy to split summer school tuitions across the two fiscal years.)

When the final results were in, the school was $2.5 million in deficit. To balance the books, the university "loaned" the school this money (with interest). Naturally, they were furious and would hold this loan against me for years after we had paid it back. But, it that year, we had accomplished many things. We had increased faculty hiring, increased compensation, and started new programs.

With the loan "jump start," we expanded the evening part-time MBA programs first to Baltimore (1999) and then a year later to Washington DC This increased the total number of evening tracks from three to five. The following year, the school launched the weekend program in Washington DC, starting with one track in 2001 and adding a second in 2002. Within a decade, we had seven part-time tracks of students whose number had grown to about 1,100.

Today, revenue sources beyond the base level of state support include market priced part-time MBA student tuition, off campus MS programs, executive education programs, center grants and contracts, private donations, and endowment proceeds. As a result, total revenues grew from about $14 million to over $65 million.

Salary Administration

The school had an excellent salary administration policy. Its process started each year with the election of a faculty salary committee. Members represented each department and each faculty rank. Because there were more departments than members of the committee, membership rotated yearly.

Every faculty member prepared an annual report detailing that member's published research for the year, his or her teaching record, and his or her service to the school. The committee then ranked each on a 1.0 to 4.0 scale, with 4.0 being the highest achievable score. The three individual rankings were then combined into a single score by weighting research as 50%, teaching as 25%, and service as 25%. The weightings demonstrated the value of research, which counted twice as much as either teaching or service. Faculty acted accordingly.

The next step depended on the amount of money allocated by the university for annual raises. The total amount constituted the "raise pool." Seventy five percent of the raise pool was given to the salary committee for its distribution to the faculty. The dean's office kept the remainder in a discretionary raise pool. The salary committee's pool was distributed by formula depending on the annual faculty rankings. The dean's pool was used to compensate for market conditions.

The process was quite fair but suffered from one major limitation. The dean's pool didn't have enough money to adjust salaries to bring them in line with the market.

Growing Faculty Salaries

Nearly every one of our professors was underpaid compared to their peers at other universities. There were few dollars to support research during the summer, so faculty taught summer courses to earn extra money. Consequently, they had less time for research.

Great business schools are invariably great at research. They also pay their faculty very well. We did neither.

Two of our goals were to bring salaries in line with top schools and to increase summer research support. Both goals would need the money that would flow from our new part-time MBA programs. I made a public pledge to the faculty: We would bring salaries to the level of the best schools within three years. I also began adding $100,000 per summer to our research fund. The fund, originally $150,000, would triple in five years.

We built a table listing every professor, ranking them in terms of research productivity and teaching quality, current salary and target salary. We calculated target salaries by using salary data from the AACSB. It was much easier to establish target salaries than to actually get a faculty member the additional money. In good years the university allocated to each school a raise budget pool of about 2–2.5%. All raises had to come out of this pool, so if I wanted to give a professor a 5% raise, another professor would have to get nothing.

There was one loophole. Suppose a professor left the school, creating what was called an "open line." Normally, the school would hold the line until a replacement was recruited. This might take a year or more, so for that time, the school would have the departed faculty member's salary to spend. I learned that it was perfectly legitimate to include the salary in the annual raises. This was usually not done because the school needed the money to hire a replacement. I added the extra dollars to the dean's discretionary raise pool.

After the salary committee did its work, my senior associate dean and I would meet with the chair of each department. We would review every faculty member's performance, marketability, and salary. We would first correct any disagreement that the department chair might have with the salary committee's recommendation. The department chair would present recommended raises that we would debate. We would then add a significant amount to highly performing and highly marketable faculty.

We were expecting rapid growth in revenues and would be able to hire new faculty from our new resources. So we transferred all available open line funds into the raise pool and gave about twenty professors an average of 14.9% raises during my first year as dean.

It took us four years (not three) to meet the salary goals. I had forgotten that salaries at other schools would be growing too so that the salary targets moved every year. We used the salary adjustment methodology throughout my term as dean.

Not only did we reach our goals, but the faculty became my greatest supporters. I had promised to take care of them and I had delivered. (After using the open line transfer technique for years, the university woke up, decided that they didn't like the power it gave deans with money, and imposed total raise constraints on every school. The only school actually affected by the constraint was the business school).

Maintaining Salary Growth

State funding that is stingy in good times and draconian in recessions afflicts Maryland and Smith, like many public institutions. This meant that in good years we might expect raise budgets of about 2.5% plus 2% cost of living increases. In bad years, we would not get raises, our budgets would be cut, and we would end up giving back all that we had received in earlier years. In these years, faculty salaries were often frozen, and we had to get permission from the provost to make any changes.

Unlike professors in many fields, business professors are highly paid and highly mobile. Other schools frequently approach the best professors to move to similar but higher paid positions. We were attempting to add ten to twelve people per year. It would have been a disaster if we began losing many people because their salaries were frozen. Unlike other campus schools, the business school had the money to raise salaries, but we couldn't do so because of the salary freezes.

We adopted the following course of action: First, we proceeded with our normal faculty reviews and evaluations and calculated the raises that people would receive if we were allowed to give raises. I reasoned that adding a dollar to someone's paycheck would be appreciated as much if the dollar were added during the summer as it would if added during the normal nine-month school year. After all, I thought, when looking at an IRS W2 form for the year, the results would be the same. So, during the summer of the freeze, we adjusted faculty summer research support to add their raises. This was a one time adjustment and entirely consistent with university policy.

A few months later, I received an e-mail from the provost reporting that someone had told him that I had found a way to give people raises and asking if this was true. Since one time summer support was not a raise, I could honestly answer, "No." "Who told you that?" I asked. There was, of course, no answer.

Two years later, the freeze was over. Our revenues had continued to grow rapidly, so we had the dollars to adjust salaries. Unfortunately, I didn't have the authority. I resorted to the same strategy we'd used before: add the dollars on open lines to the raise pool and then put the dollars back on the lines when we were ready to use them. This time, I mentioned to the provost that we were going to use this technique to adjust salaries, and hearing no objection, we did so.

A few months later, the provost said to me: "I don't know whether I should be angry about this or not. Your raises averaged more than 5.5% while everyone else on campus got 2.5%. If other deans knew about this, they would be furious." I said, "I told you I was going to do this," and he responded, "But I didn't realize the magnitude."

The exchange was a good example of the mismatch between my operating style and what might have been acceptable to the university. Instead of just acting, I could have given the provost a list of the faculty to be given significant raises and the amounts of the raises. He then could have said yes or no. Theoretically he had no legitimate basis to say no, but I expected he would because other schools weren't giving such raises. So, rather than risk a turndown, I moved ahead on my own authority.

The next year, the university imposed a cap on the total raises that could be given. I'm sure that no one but me noticed. The ironic part of this episode was that throughout the freeze period, my faculty complained about their frozen salaries. They would continue to complain for years. Apparently, to them, a dollar in the summer was not the same as a dollar during the school year.

Hiring People

If you come from the commercial world, the academic hiring process seems bizarre. As in industry, the first step in hiring someone is to write a job description. In industry, you then advertise for candidates, interview those with the best responses, and hire someone. In academia, the dean appoints a search committee to solicit applications and interview people. We were required to appoint "balanced" committees with sexual and racial diversity. Also, the school was required to have an equity officer who was a member of all searches. The equity officer had to sign off on a search plan for every search and also sign off on the results of the search.

Non-academic hires were the most cumbersome. A search was designated to run over a specified time, after which the search would be closed and the top few candidates selected for interviews. If the ideal candidate walked in the door before the end of the search, we could not hire the person because the search was still open. The group of candidates had to be diverse, independent of the actual merits of the candidate pool. If we didn't have enough diversity, we might be required to reopen the search. If you knew a great candidate for a job, you couldn't just hire the person. You would have to set up a search and a search committee and go through the entire process. By its end, the original candidate you wanted might no longer be available.

If we were hiring for a position reporting to me, I was not allowed to review the applications and resumes of the candidate pool. I was only able to review those of the candidates selected at the end. The hiring process might take up to six months, with many good candidates withdrawing because they had been offered jobs by other institutions.

I complained about the inefficiency of the hiring process a number of times and suggested that we set up an experiment to expedite it. My suggestion was turned down.

Hiring academics was a bit better because the academic world operates on an academic calendar, with candidates graduating and being hired to start work in the fall semester. We would need to create a search committee for each position being hired. Our faculty would attend major conferences where graduating candidates would be interviewed and selected for on campus visits. On campus interviewing might start in the fall or winter for hiring the next summer or fall. We might invite three or four candidates to Maryland for each position. I would interview each one to give them a clear picture of our vision. Excellent prospects could receive many offers, and therefore we would often have to increase the salaries offered or the concessions made to get the very best ones.

Hiring for major university positions such as vice presidents was more elaborate. I chaired several searches and served on several other search committees. The search committee could contain as many as fifteen to twenty individuals drawn from around the campus and from the alumni. Meetings were very formal, but the mechanisms used to sort candidates varied from committee to committee. One committee allowed me (the chairman) to sort resumes and reject the most obviously unqualified. Another committee insisted that everyone review and discuss every application received. The time wasted by the second approach threatened to drive me crazy, but I survived, and in both cases, we selected reasonable finalists.

Improving Teaching Quality

One of the school's goals was "to provide a superb teaching environment." The school's teaching quality was anything but superb. There were a number of excellent teachers, but on the whole, teaching was not a very high priority. To their credit, the faculty had adopted a teaching rating process. The students rated every course along a number of dimensions, and an overall rating from 1.0–5.0 was calculated. (4.0 and above was considered excellent.) Every semester, the ratings were collected into a book that a few people may have reviewed but did nothing to follow up.

I began to review the ratings of every teacher in every course. I would note the excellent reviews and the poor ones (3.5 and below.) I began sending e-mail notes to the department chairs about the poor ones, asking what had happened and what they planned to do about it. I would send congratulatory e-mails to faculty with high ratings. Soon the message became clear: The dean was interested in teaching quality.

I then introduced questions about teaching quality in our annual department strategic planning sessions. Some departments responded by their own analyses of teaching quality and created tables of their teaching performance against other departments. I directed each department to create a plan to improve the quality of one to two courses per year. This was a modest goal but one that would have cumulative results. The departments responded.

I reinforced the teaching quality message by refusing to sanction the promotion of an associate professor to full professor because of poor teaching. This message was like a cannon explosion. The dean was really serious about teaching quality.

Over the course of a decade, teaching quality soared. From an average of less than 4.0 across all courses and faculty, teaching ratings grew to over 4.25 for the school, with many faculty garnering 4.5 or higher ratings. To be promoted at Smith, a professor had to be a superb researcher and an excellent teacher!

Travels of a Dean

After I was appointed the next dean of the Maryland Business School, I completed my appointment with DARPA and left for a six-week vacation with my wife. Our itinerary included Papua New Guinea, Fiji, Australia, and New Zealand.

Our first stop was Port Moresby in New Guinea. We would fly from there to a small regional airport on the Sepik River. We would then ride down the river in a flat-bottomed boat for about four hours to meet a riverboat visiting native tribes on the river's banks. We would eat and sleep on the boat and take excursions to the tribes during the day. It would be a grand adventure.

During dinner of the second night on the boat, we departed from the planned schedule. The door to the outside burst open and hooded men waving guns and machetes took us captive. They took our money, robbed the boat's safe, and started breaking up the boat for its valuable parts.

An arrow slammed into the door, and gunshots chased the pirates into their boats. A native tribe armed with bows and arrows had rescued us. They stood guard over the boat for the rest of the night. The next day we departed for safer parts.

The remainder of our trip was less eventful, but I started at Maryland with a "can you top this story." I also sent a postcard to my least favorite DARPA executive. It said: "Captured by pirates and rescued by a tribe of natives. Wish you were here!"

I hadn't thought about the travel that would be required for the dean's position. During my days at DARPA and running companies, most of my business travel was domestic. At Maryland, there were lots of domestic trips to various deans' meetings and to meet with potential donors. For example, I was in St. Louis on 9/11 and spent two days getting home in a rented limousine. There were an increasing number of international trips.

We had a partnership with a school in Poland, the University of Lotz (pronounced 'woodge.') Lotz's business school operated a "Polish-American" center, with Maryland being the American partner. My wife and I were invited to visit the university and participate in their EMBA graduate ceremonies, where I would be their keynote speaker. The people were wonderful and the food was great. I also won the crowd by sharing that my grandmother had been from Poland and I had had "Grandmother's Soup" for lunch at a local restaurant. It was chicken soup.

My wife and I would visit London for a week's vacation once a year. Could I be interviewed by the Financial Times while I was there? "Of course" was the answer.

I was appointed to the International Academy of Management and elected its Vice Chairman for the Americas. Could I drop by Barcelona, Spain, where an Academy meeting was taking place while I was in London? And while I was there, could I stay for an extra day and give a speech to alumni in Barcelona and Madrid (via videoconferencing)? As usual, the answer was "yes."

I had met the Governor of Maryland when he had visited the business school and also when he had agreed to provide $6 million for Van Munching Hall's addition. He participated in the formal groundbreaking for the new wing. After an election, there was a new governor. I received an invitation to go to Singapore and China with the governor and a twenty-four-person trade delegation. By that time

I had realized that knowing the governor was a good idea for a dean. I wanted to meet the new governor, so I decided to go.

The governor's itinerary was to fly nonstop from Newark Airport to Singapore and then to go to Shanghai and Beijing. It took me about six hours to get from my home in Virginia to Newark, but I was able to get on the same airplane as the governor, a Singapore Airlines flight. Early the next day (after fifteen hours in the air), when people were being served breakfast, I introduced myself to the governor and his chief of staff. We traded a few polite words, and I proffered an invitation for the governor to speak at the Smith School.

The trade delegates were swept through Singapore customs and immigration without delay and loaded on a bus. The governor, his chief, and security guards led in a limousine. The first stop was a hotel to freshen up. Then we rushed to a meeting with the Governor of Singapore and a large group of government and business officials. At the meeting, the governor introduced us and asked us each to say a few words. I spoke about the importance of globalization and the importance of the Far East in globalization.

The governor must have liked what he heard because he asked me to sit next to him at a lunch meeting with Singapore business executives. Thereafter, he invited me to ride with him in his limousine. He would ask me to speak at all of our meetings including a large CEO awards banquet. At that banquet, I sat at the head table and was asked to come on stage to help hand out awards. I was given plaques and asked to hand them to the recipients. Unfortunately, the awards were in Chinese, which I couldn't read, so probably I handed plaques to the wrong people. No matter, it was fun!

By the third day, I was going out to private dinners with the governor and we had become very friendly. Later this would be very important because it helped me to secure state funding for part of our North Wing expansion.

It was a fabulous trip. I found Shanghai and Beijing to be wonderful cities. In the next few years, I would return six times.

Years later, on an airplane returning home from London, I calculated that I had been on an international trip every two months over a several year period: Zurich three times, Tunisia, Barcelona twice, Beijing five times, Shanghai six times, London countless times, Paris and Cannes, New Delhi, Holland, Singapore, and Tokyo.

Being a member of the AACSB Board required 3–4 trips per year to board meetings. After my board duties were complete, I was appointed to its Accreditation Maintenance Committee. This meant traveling to meetings twice a year and also chairing accreditation reviews at different universities. Each review involved a three-day trip to the school under review. I chaired reviews at Wisconsin, Indiana, Boston University, Bentley College, and the Korean Advanced Institute of Science and Technology. We also had semi-annual meetings in Chicago of a group of deans constituting a "large public business schools" peer group. During these half-day meetings we would report on our schools' activities and also share data. The meetings were held at the O'Hare airport hotel so we could arrive in the morning and leave for home in the afternoon.

The Rankings

Business schools are blessed and cursed by magazines and newspapers that have learned that rankings sell magazines. Among the business school rankings are annual publications by *Business Week* (BW), *the Financial Times* (FT), and *U.S. News and World Reports* (USN). Many others also have published their version of ratings, such as *Forbes, Computer World, the Wall Street Journal,* and *the Economist.* There are ratings for undergraduate programs, MBA programs, EMBA programs, part-time programs, and non-degree educational programs.

The editors of each publication have decided that they alone know how to measure a business school's quality. Some ratings systems tabulate the opinions of business school administrators (like USN's undergraduate rating system) and are therefore popularity contests. Others collect data from students regarding job offers and student scores on the Graduate Management Aptitude Test (GMAT). Many ask the individual schools being ranked to supply the data to be used in the calculations. Others survey a school's potential employers and ask them about their favorite schools.

All of the ranking systems have major flaws that don't seem to bother their publishers. Systems based on reputation tend to favor the older, larger schools such as Harvard and Wharton. Who is going to say something bad about them? Systems that use salaries are biased towards that same group of schools and towards schools that place students into high paying fields such as finance and consulting. Schools that place students into government positions and low wage areas do not fare well on salary measures. Also, students tend to get paid more with graduate degrees from schools like Harvard and Wharton because they were getting higher salaries before they started their graduate programs.

The *Financial Times* includes a return on investment (ROI) criterion in its ranking. Even though they have the largest salaries, the schools ranked the highest by *U.S. News and World Reports* have the lowest ROIs!

Some publishers, like USN, include student selectivity and student GMATs in their rating systems. FT includes faculty research when ranking MBA programs. BW has an "intellectual quotient" component in its ranking.

In my opinion, the poorest of the major MBA rankings is the one published by USN. This ranking has a reputation component, a student selectivity component, a job placement component, and a salary component. The business schools themselves submit much of the data used. The ranking is strongly biased towards well established, well known schools that get higher numbers of applications from candidates with higher starting salaries. (The irony that I've quoted USN's rankings in this text as well as many times in public has not escaped me.)

Submitting data that will be used in rankings places tremendous ethical pressure on deans. Students, alumni, and employers treat rankings as gospel. A drop in the rankings can create a crisis in the dean's office. It's easy to make mistakes or cook the books when submitting data. I didn't think of this until one day when I was shocked by a plunge in our USN MBA rankings. Rather than sit quietly, I published the following on our website:

> I recently opened an e-mail from *US News and World Reports* (*USN*) indicating that our MBA program ranking dropped from #29 to #43. My initial reaction, shock, turned to frustration and anger after examining the business school submitted data on which much of the USN survey is based. I have been tracking business school submissions of this data for other magazine and newspaper surveys because of their impact on the rankings. In particular, data about most of the schools surveyed by USN are also available on the Business Week Online (BW) and Financial Times (FT) websites. Given the need for strong business ethics, you can imagine my distress when comparing these submissions to realize that there are significant discrepancies in the way many schools have reported.
>
> A critical element of the survey is recruiter related data including the percentage of students accepting offers by graduation and within ninety days after graduation. There are very specific standards about how these data must be reported. Here are some obvious examples of inconsistent reporting for four of the top 25 USN ranked schools:
>
> School A told BW that 93% of their students were seeking jobs and that 62% and 74% had received offers by graduation and by 90 days after graduation. They told USN that of the students seeking jobs, 77.6% and 89.6% had accepted offers by graduation or within 90 days after graduation. There is no way that these two sets of numbers can both be true. They also told the Financial Times that the percentage of students accepting offers within 90 days was 83%.
>
> School B reported to USN that the percentage of students accepting offers within 90 days after graduation was

85.8% but they told the FT that 78% of their graduates had accepted offers within the same 90 days.

School C gave USN 87.7% and 94.8% for the acceptance numbers while they told BW that the percentages of job offers were 72% at graduation and 76% within 90 days. Analysis of the numbers seeking employment data on the BW website indicates that these two different sets cannot be consistent.

School D reported 90 days after graduation acceptances to USN as 92% but reported to FT that 84% had accepted offers.

While there may be perfectly good explanations for some of these discrepancies, there were also many others variances in other schools' submissions and because of these variances, one must question the validity of the overall USN rankings (or other rankings).

We were not the only school whose rankings were affected. Other major point spread drops included one school dropping from #35 to #46, another from #33 to #43 and a third from #41 to #49. Even Washington University in St. Louis dropped from #26 to #31. On the other hand, many schools benefited. One went from #44 to #29 and two others each jumped from #30 to #24. It's impossible to predict what the actual rankings would have been if all of the schools had reported their data consistently. But, the key question is, **is it plausible that the quality of so many schools could change so significantly in one year?**

What can be done to insure more reliable results in the future? We would like to see that the magazines and newspaper ranking organizations not accept data unless schools are willing to open themselves to audit. We would like to create a committee of deans with the right to challenge questionable submissions and request independent audits for such submissions. Will this happen? I can't guarantee it but magazines such as FT have already announced plans to audit some data and the AACSB International has a project to collect auditable data that could become the official source of all national rankings.

In the meantime, regardless of what happens in the future, we are stuck for the next year with a #43 ranking from one survey. How should we deal with this? First, if you seek external validation, look at the other major surveys. Just last month, FT ranked us #21 in the US with the #3 best ROI for students among the top schools. Last year, the *Wall Street Journal* ranked us #13. BW ranks us #27. And, as absurd as it may seem to refer to the USN survey, the USN specialty rankings (based on surveys of deans and MBA directors) rated our part time MBA program #13 (up from #20 last year), Management Information Systems #9, Entrepreneurship #15 (from #19 last year), General Management #23, International Business #23, and Production/Operations Management #26. So what ranking should you believe: #13, #21, #27, or #43? Take your pick.

The most important fact is that the school is no different in quality today than it was two days ago. We are a fine institution. Our faculty, students, staff, alumni and programs are proof of this. We have a great academic program, tremendous teaching quality and are a leader in business school research. And, we have a collaborative and vital student body that is as good as any on earth. We are not perfect but we know our areas of weakness, have committed the funds and human resources to work on them and are constantly making progress.

In just two months, we begin occupying our new wing with significant upgrades in all facilities including a major new Career Management Center. We are expanding our alumni and career center staffs in accordance with MBA student recommendations. "Building the Smith Community" is a key initiative in our strategic plan. This summer, we are introducing a new post-graduate summer career program. We have entered into a matching grants partnership to expand internship opportunities for students. We are acting now to insure that regardless of how other schools report their numbers, we will continue to build on our current excellence. And, we will do all of this with integrity and accurate reporting.

As of this writing, only one publication (FT) attempts to audit business school submissions. I shared my findings of inaccuracies in data with a BW editor. She did her own analysis, found more discrepancies, and told me that she would write an article about the problem. Six months later I asked her how the article was coming. She responded: "My editors killed the story because if we questioned one ranking system, it exposed the others, including ours, to questions."

Most business school deans hate the rankings because they don't measure quality but expose the schools to all types of questions and criticisms. It's like reading the sports pages on Monday morning and finding that the games you watched on Sunday had different outcomes than the ones you remember. I hate the rankings too.

Chapter 4

Change Comes from Within

Accreditation

In January 2006, we published this announcement:

Smith School Receives Praise from
AACSB International in Review Process

After an intense process, the review by AACSB International is complete and the Smith School has been accredited for another five years. In the report, the strengths and effective practices commended are:

1. Dean Frank has provided dynamic, entrepreneurial leadership that has led to growth in programs and generated significant new financial resources for the Smith School.
2. The growth and development of the school has been guided by a best in class strategic planning process.
3. The school has established a consistent brand—"Leaders for the Digital Economy"—that builds from its strengths and distinctive competencies.
4. The netcentric research labs—i.e. supply chain, financial markets, electronic markets, behavioral—create an integrated research and teaching environment used by faculty and students across the school's programs.

5. The Smith School has adopted a process for developing research centers focused on interdisciplinary issues rooted in the concerns of the school's academic departments.

If the accreditation review had taken place a few years earlier, the results might have been very different. In AACSB's words:

> AACSB provides internationally recognized, specialized accreditation for business and accounting programs at the bachelor's, master's, and doctoral level. The AACSB Accreditation Standards challenge post-secondary educators to pursue excellence and continuous improvement throughout their business programs. AACSB Accreditation is known, worldwide, as the longest standing, most recognized form of specialized/professional accreditation an institution and its business programs can earn.

Of the more than 2,000 business schools and programs, about 400 have AACSB accreditation. To be accredited, a school must meet certain eligibility standards; must have continuous improvement plans; and must meet a set of performance standards on student admission and retention, student support, the sufficiency of faculty for the number of students being taught, and faculty qualifications, management, and support. Accredited schools are revisited every five years, after which accreditation can be reaffirmed, suspended, or revoked.

Recall that at the start of my deanship, we were flooded with undergraduate students who were taught by adjuncts. Our courses did not have the faculty coverage required by the AACSB. Even though I alerted the provost to this problem many times, he was not sympathetic. The university did nothing to help us correct the problem. We saved the day by hiring teaching professors and additional faculty, paid for by the expansion of part-time and executive MBAs. Without this expansion, the story might have had a different ending—the suspension of Maryland's business accreditation. At that point, someone outside the business school might have cared!

Innovative Programming

In 1998, the school began a comprehensive restructuring of the MBA program to introduce curriculum innovation and distinctiveness. A portfolio of programs with significant scheduling, geographic, and delivery flexibility was put in place. Elective offerings were redesigned and introduced the following fall. The new program included scheduling options for full-time and fully employed students and offerings across multiple part-time tracks. Expansion of program options across time and location assured access to the very best members of the candidate pool.

The curriculum was transformed along the technological lines outlined in the initial strategic plan. Following the redesign of the electives options, an entirely new MBA core was developed and implemented. Resources to strengthen the school's technology infrastructure were increased. The school hired a chief technology officer for the school, and expenditures for staff and technology infrastructure more than tripled. The school developed laboratories in supply chain and financial markets and rolled out five centers—Supply Chain Management; E-Service; Electronic Markets and Enterprises; and Human Capital, Technology, and Innovation—aimed at supporting research at the intersection of business and technology.

Each center was created with pilot funding for three years from the dean's office, with the expectation that the centers would be self-sufficient thereafter. Funded, center-based research has expanded from virtually $0 to about $5 million, but the centers never achieved my ultimate goal for them—to provide major training grounds for students along with significant partnerships with industry and government. I had seen this work when visiting Wisconsin's business school, but no matter how much I talked about it at Maryland, we made very little progress in this direction.

Balancing the Books

When I first became dean, I asked to see a copy of the school's budget. I was given a single typewritten page with a few handwritten notes listing a series of expenses. Our business manager stared blankly at me when I asked: "How are we doing against the budget?" As I delved deeper, I discovered that there was no monthly or quarterly reconciliation and that no one in the financial management department could answer meaningful questions about the school's accounts. Many of our managers had no concept of a budget, and no one understood the school's cash flows. Indeed, cash flow seemed to be a foreign word.

The chief financial manager (with the formal title of "business manager") had no formal training in accounting. The university's financial system was not structured to produce conventional Profit and Loss reports. Most accounts didn't even have the capability of booking revenues so that, for example, if we were reimbursed for copying costs, the reimbursement was entered as a negative expense. This meant that I couldn't get the answer to even the simple question: "How much are we spending on copying?" Not being able to get answers to simple finance questions literally drove me crazy, and I wasted huge amounts of time trying to train the staff to answer them.

The situation went from serious to absurd when I learned that there were many "off budget" expenses that never went through the school's accounts. Some expenses were paid by the university's foundation using monies contributed by alumni and other donors. Business personnel couldn't access some of our accounts in the university's financial systems. And, no one had ever produced a Profit and Loss statement that had any relevance to our operations.

My first attempts to install budgeting went nowhere. It turned out that people had accounts at the University of Maryland Foundation. If they needed extra money, they would draw it from the foundation without my knowledge. I had a confrontation with my senior associate dean about a foundation account of about $100,000 for our Quest program. (Actually it was a shouting match, with me yelling, "It's not their money. It's mine!")

This had been a donation to help start the program, and they had treated the account like their own piggy bank. To gain control, I had to order that no one could draw on foundation monies without my prior authorization. There was culture shock over this action since people viewed the foundation accounts as their money and not the school's.

In addition to the University of Maryland foundation, the business school operated a small foundation. I tried to get an idea of the available cash in this foundation, but no one could give it to me. I finally asked to see the cash balances for the last year and reasoned that the minimum monthly balance represented the amount of cash we didn't need. I appropriated excess monies for use by the business school.

I examined every account in the Maryland foundation and again appropriated balances for my use. In these ways I discovered over $500,000 of available dollars. This was a huge amount relative the size of the school, which at that time had a budget of around $14 million.

I was running an operation without any of the usual financial tools needed to manage a business. The absurdity of the situation did not occur to me at the time, but I wondered why the previous dean, who had been an industry financial executive, hadn't tackled financial reporting for the school. I set out to build the tools but quickly learned that I couldn't do so without trained people. After my initial training efforts failed, I asked the business manager to leave the school and hired an individual as assistant dean who came from the commercial world. She in turn replaced the entire finance staff.

Because the university systems and procedures were arcane, inefficient, and in many cases, outright stupid, and we had a group of new staff, we had a series of disasters before we began to conquer the system. One such disaster involved many of the faculty falling out of the university payroll system and not being paid at the beginning of the semester. Another disaster was even more serious.

In an effort to find out more about the school's assets and revenues, I met with the university's Foundation finance vice president to review the school's accounts at the Foundation. We went through a detailed list of accounts with annual payouts totaling about $1 million.

After the review, I asked the question: "So therefore, I can expect to get $1 million at the beginning of the next fiscal year?" I was shocked by her answer: "No, we've already advanced you this money."

I sat stunned but didn't say anything except thank you for the information and goodbye. When I left her office I was actually shaking. My business manager was balancing the books by using next year's monies. Therefore the school was operating at a deficit. What was worse, since I wouldn't continue to borrow from the future, I would be short $1 million for the coming fiscal year.

The next week, in my monthly meeting with the provost, I told him what I had learned. I added: "In the world I come from, people get fired or go to jail for doing this." He didn't say anything. He had no advice and didn't offer to help. I was on my own!

Procuring an Accounting System

I was in my office reviewing the hopeless nature of our attempt to generate adequate financial information. My new chief financial officer told me: "We need to install a financial system. But we can't. It would take us two years for the (university's) procurement department to procure one for us. We would have to write a specification; they would review it, rewrite it, write a request for procurement, and then undertake a formal procurement. Each step would take at least six months."

"What would you like to do?" I asked. "Just buy one," was the response. "For example, here's one that would do the job for $25,000. But we can't buy it because my husband sells these systems and it would be a conflict for me to be involved."

I called my senior associate dean into my office and asked him (he happened to be a lawyer): "Do you see anything wrong with you buying this?" His response, "No," was followed by my direction: "Buy it!"

A few months later the system was installed and producing financial reports. I was in heaven. But it didn't last. There are no good deeds in academia. Apparently, the university's finance people didn't want schools to have their own accounting systems. (Later I discovered that the engineering school had built one for themselves.) I was called to the provost's office, informed that I had violated university policy, handed a draft latter accusing me of financial irresponsibility (the school's deficit), and accused of imperiling the university and virtually everything except crimes against humanity. "Review this letter," the provost directed me, "and make whatever changes are necessary."

Back at the business school I reviewed the letter. I was appalled by what I read. It was a biased set of accusations against my staff and me. Editing this letter would be a no-win proposition. I called the provost and told him that I refused to either rewrite or accept the letter since it was a gross misrepresentation of the facts. I sent him a detailed description of the issues. Here's what I outlined:

FRANK'S NOTES ON B-SCHOOL ACCOUNTING

Initial Financial Condition

- School's operating condition misrepresented to candidates for my dean's position.
- Structural deficit hidden.
- Limitations in the accounting system caused the "Gift Accounts" to become an amalgam of activities, many unrelated to the label "Gifts."
- Normal 4th quarter operating mechanism funded deficits in state operating accounts with large transfers of Foundation monies.
- University practices made it impossible to accurately analyze costs. For example, funds transferred to the business school were transferred as offsets to costs, resulting in an artificially low picture of operating expenses.
- School's personnel practices inadequate. Personnel assigned to incorrect lines, split between lines, or in the wrong departments.

Approach

- Attempted to train Business Manager and develop improved reporting procedures
- Directed hiring additional financial staff and attempted to build appropriate operation.
- Removed Financial Manager and initiated outside search (with head-hunter).
- Directed the development of improved accounting processes requiring rebuilding entire organization and processes from scratch.
- Ceased inappropriate funding and reporting mechanisms.
- Hidden deficit emerged.
- Entire department rebuilt, financial processes overhauled, bottom-up budgeting and reporting installed.

Status

- First bottom-up operating budget in school's history.
- Monthly reporting to operating units.
- Personnel practices revised.
- All employees correctly reclassified in budget categories.
- Long range (5-Year) forecast based on actual financial data
- Still to be done:
  - Better expense management
  - Better contract management
  - Improved planning

A few days later I received a watered down version of the original letter. Also, I met with the President to give him the facts. He ordered me to remove our accounting system and procure one through official channels. I could, however, continue to operate our system until a new one was installed. At no time did anyone in the university's administration acknowledge to me the validity of my analysis or the university's responsibility for allowing the mess to take place.

Back at the business school, I met with my chief financial officer and gave her the bad news. "We need to procure a new system. Write up a specification and send it over to Procurement. Then do nothing! It will take years for them to act. Send it to them but don't talk to them about it unless they call you."

Two years later we still hadn't heard from Procurement. When asked by the President what had happened, I responded, "It's in Procurement." I had to bite the insides of my cheeks to keep from smiling. He said nothing!

The Financial Model

It began simply. I created a spreadsheet of the revenues and costs of the school. It had two worksheets: one for revenue, the second for costs. My first attempt was inaccurate because I didn't understand the revenue flows and their splits with the university and also didn't have a very good understanding of costs.

As the months went on, my data became more accurate but our needs became greater. I tried to project the income from our part-time programs. This required that I know the number of students taking courses as well as the number of courses they would be taking each semester. We didn't have this data in any useful form.

We had to analyze each university account to determine the adjustments to costs caused by recording revenues as negative costs. We were slowly able to get a more accurate sense of our operating costs.

If the school were relatively static, a high level analysis would have been sufficient. But we were anything but static. We were projecting significant faculty hiring, expansion of facilities, and many other expenditures. We began building separate spreadsheets for each. There was one for faculty hiring, one for building debt, and another to model revenues from the part-time programs by year. The last included projections of tuition by year along with a projection of the number of students.

The spreadsheets were becoming difficult to use because we needed to link many of them together. My chief administrative officer saved the day by integrating them into a single spreadsheet model.

This model evolved from a relatively simple tool to a sophisticated planning model. We would update the model weekly and with the updated data, forecast our finances for the next five years. The model, when fully developed, had the following worksheets:

- Current year forecast and 4-year plan
- Campus support
- North Wing expenditures
- South Wing expenditures
- Debt service on original Van Munching Hall
- DC and part-time facility costs
- Hiring
- Use of gifts
- Grants
- Contingencies
- Actual to budget for the current fiscal year
- Fees
- Part-time MBA tuition
- MBA differential tuition
- EMBA tuition

In addition to weekly updates, we would reconcile the model with the outputs of our accounting system on a quarterly basis as well at the end of the academic year after the results of the year were reconciled with the university's accounts.

The model gave me a tool to investigate the impact of hiring and other expenditure decisions. I was able to vary the projected number of students as well as projected tuition increases to explore changes in revenue. We built a year-by-year forecast of revenues as a function of year-by-year tuition and fee increases. We also had a five-year faculty hiring model organized by academic departments.

This powerful planning system was, as far as I know, unique in business schools.

They Are Because They Are

In Orwell's *Animal Farm*, all animals are equal, except that pigs are more equal than others. At Maryland, all schools were equal except that some, like the engineering school, were more equal than others, and the business school was less equal. Inequalities were built into the system: the engineering school received more funding than other schools; the business school received less funding. As a consequence, we had half of the faculty and graduate assistants we needed to teach our courses.

I started investigating graduate assistant (GA) funding and quickly discovered how difficult it would be to get more money from the university. A GA is a graduate student who is paid a several thousand dollar stipend plus part of his tuition (called tuition remission) for assisting a faculty member or teaching an undergraduate class. I had difficulty understanding why our GA base was so small when we had such large requirements. So I asked the provost. His response: "It depends on the number of faculty you have." When I pointed out that our ratio of GAs to faculty members was half of the campus average, he changed his story. "Actually, it depends on the number of credit hours you teach." "But," I responded, "we teach 10% of the campus credit hours with 5% of the faculty and 6% of the graduate assistants." There was no response.

"How do I change this?" I asked. "You have to talk to the dean of the graduate school," was the response. So I met with the dean of the graduate school, showed him the numbers, and asked how to get more money. "I can't do it. That's the job of APAC (a committee made up of faculty from around the campus.) You have to speak with the provost."

Returning to the provost, I reported the conversation, got no advice on how to proceed, and left his office with the conclusion that we weren't getting more graduate assistant funding. APAC was a black hole made up of campus faculty. No university faculty committee would vote to give the business school more money. APAC would be a dead end.

I decided to find out how a GA was appointed. I found that individual schools had the authority to appoint GAs. All we had to do was give a student a letter appointing him or her for a year. The campus automatically paid tuition remission and the school paid the GA's salary (called a stipend). Normally, this was $5,000 or $10,000 depending on whether the student worked 10 or 20 hours per week for the school.

To increase the number of GAs, we would need the money to pay the stipends. I had confidence in our revenue projections and our ability to pay. We wanted fifty additional graduate assistants. I decided to add ten per year for five years, costing us $50,000 the first year and $250,000 by the fifth. I was sure that at the campus level, no one would notice (they didn't). The moral: You can't change the system. You need to find the holes and cracks in the system and exploit these openings.

Speeches, Speeches, and More Speeches

Everyone wanted the dean. If there was an interesting person visiting the school, I would be asked to spend a few minutes with him or her. If there was visiting group, I would be asked to welcome them. If an alumni meeting was being held, I would be asked to host it, give a welcome address, and spend time with the attendees.

New York, Baltimore, Washington, College Park, Seattle, San Francisco, and Tampa—I was there, hosting, speaking, talking, and mingling. Some days I would open a breakfast with a welcome speech, rush off to a meeting, be back at my desk by 10:00 a.m., work for two hours, and then rush to welcome another group at lunch. The agenda might be repeated two or three times a week, with the remaining days spent on funds raising trips, at deans' conferences, or visiting corporations to promote the school.

At the end of a semester, I presided over our graduation ceremonies. I was the commencement speaker at foreign universities—Poland, Switzerland, Beijing, Shanghai, and Tunisia were all recipients of my words. I was invited to speak at many others. Back home, there were MBA breakfasts, lunches, and dinners. I would have breakfasts with groups of undergraduates. Every spring, we would have open houses and receptions for admitted graduate students. In the fall, there were "Welcome to Smith" receptions. I would kick off all of these with a speech about the future of the Smith School.

After joining the AACSB board, I became active in their workshops and conferences. This meant organizing or chairing sessions at AACSB meetings. My most significant was developing the plenary session at an AACSB annual meeting. The topic—"business school models"—described three different business school systems: private, public, and for profit. I invited the dean of Columbia's business school to present their model of a private school. A senior representative presented the University of Phoenix's private model. I presented the Smith School public model. It was a major coup since I was able to explain to nearly all current business school deans what we were doing and where we were going.

I was invited to attend the annual meeting of the Midatlantic Association for the Advancement of Business Schools (MAACBA) to give a speech on supply chain management. I was then asked to join MAACBA's executive committee as second vice president. I was told the position didn't require much work. What I wasn't told was that the following year, I would become first vice president and program chair. In that capacity I would have to organize and chair the annual meeting. The following year I would become the president of the association. We held that year's annual meeting at the Smith School. About one hundred faculty and administrators from throughout the midatlantic region attended. It was a fabulous success.

After a while, I could give speeches in my sleep or given a topic one minute, I could produce a polished presentation the next.

We Discover Financing

The operations of the business school were a shambles.Administrative support was absent, financial management was a mystery, and computer support was performed by amateurs. Our infrastructure was obsolete. Computers were old and broken, printers didn't work, e-mail was erratic, and support was a fiction.

The average faculty member had an old computer that couldn't run either his classroom or research models.There was little prospect of near term fixes because the school could only afford to replace about 25% of the aging computers in any one year.

The situation was hopeless until I asked whether we could lease new computers. It turned out that we could.We did so, and six months later, the school had all new computers in its classrooms and faculty offices.Amazingly enough, even though we were in a business school, no one had thought of financing.

A High School Marching Band—We Will Be Mediocre

Nearly every day one or more faculty members would come to my office to complain about the inefficiency of our support. I could see this myself when I found students wandering the halls with blank stares after having been sent from office to office to get something done.

After a particularly egregious example, I told one professor that I was aware of the problem and that my goal was to turn our support people into a precision drill team. He countered, "How about a high school marching band." I thought for a second and then agreed. "A high school marching band plays a recognizable tune, and they all get to the end of the field at about the same time."

"That will be our near term goal. Our goal will be to become mediocre. Once we are mediocre, we will shoot for good. But one day, we will be great!"

It took years. We reached our goal of mediocrity and changed the goal to "good." When we became good, we adopted a new goal—"excellence." After excellence would come "great."

Teaching Professors—a New Model

A young assistant professor pleaded with me: "I don't know what is going to happen to me. No one will tell me whether I have a chance at tenure. I am not a very good researcher but I am one of our best teachers. I may have to leave the school in a year if I don't get tenure."

"In the world I come from," I told her, "we don't throw people away who are great at one thing but aren't great at another. We build teams." I promised her I would look into the situation.

Teaching ranks in a typical university are made up of tenured and tenured track professors, lecturers, adjuncts, and graduate students. Tenured professors are the elite. Adjuncts sit at the bottom of the hierarchy, teaching an occasional course for a pittance. Adjuncts usually work full-time for a different organization and have little allegiance to the teaching institution. They come and they go. Some may be good teachers, but even those have little time to spend with students. None of them have contact with the permanent faculty and may know little or nothing about the school. There is little or no quality control.

I had been an adjunct professor at Wharton, so I know first hand the shortcomings of the position.

Lecturers are typically full-time employees of the school who are hired on an annual basis. In many schools, a lecturer may not know until April or May whether or not he will have a job next September. Adequate lecturers tend to get rehired, but because of the limitations of the system, they have little association with the school. They are not treated like faculty and therefore aren't part of the school's culture. Schools that don't have enough full-time professors meet their teaching need with adjuncts and lecturers.

The system is driven by economics because few schools can afford to staff all of their teaching requirements with full-time faculty. The system stinks with students suffering.

I had promised to look into the assistant professor's problem. Along the way, I discovered that the school was drowning in adjuncts of uneven quality, and there was no easy fix. A fix would take radical thinking.

Top business schools were on a path towards self-destruction. Professors were getting paid more and more for teaching less and less. There was no way that a school like Maryland could meet its teaching needs by hiring only tenure track faculty. It would cost too much, and there weren't enough quality teachers and researchers on the market who could be hired even if we had the money.

Suppose, I wondered, we could hire superb teachers who had no research responsibilities. They would teach twice as many courses as the tenured faculty but in nearly every respect, they would have the same rights and privileges as the tenured people. To build an allegiance to the school, we would give them long-term employment contracts and call them "teaching professors" to indicate their high rank within the school.

The danger was that if all we wanted was to build a fine teaching school, we could hire only teaching professors. If teaching professors crowded out the tenure track, our research would diminish. To keep research and teaching balanced, we would limit the number of teaching professors to 10–15% of any department's total faculty.

I described the concept to the faculty. We agreed to proceed as an experiment. Each department would be allowed to hire one teaching professor. We would evaluate the outcome in a year or two.

Teaching Professors by Another Name

Teaching professors were a huge success. We hired the assistant professor responsible for my idea as a TP. She was given a larger teaching load and more responsibility. Another department hired a visiting professor as a TP. That hire turned out to be a brilliant teacher and a good colleague. A third professor came to me with the request to convert from the tenure track to a teaching professor. He told me that he liked research but he loved teaching. I approved the conversion.

Within a couple of years, teaching professors had made a visible improvement in our teaching quality and weak adjuncts were being replaced. It was time to institutionalize the TP concept by adopting a faculty resolution defining TPs as "faculty" and formalizing their rights and obligations. The way to do this was to change the school's "constitution" to include teaching professors.

At Maryland, every academic unit has a constitution approved by the unit's faculty and ratified by the university's Senate. The Senate is a pseudo governing body made up of faculty and staff elected by the units. It is also an agent for the status quo because getting changes approved by the Senate is a time consuming and erratic process.

To change a school's constitution, the change must first be proposed to the entire faculty and then, at a later meeting, two thirds of the faculty must approve the change. I appointed a committee to study the TP position and to define its qualifications, rights, and responsibilities. The committee developed a thoughtful response. The general requirement of the TP position would be:

General Qualifications of a Teaching Professor
    PhD or equivalent, teaching excellence, service excellence
    Strong and collegial contribution to the school
Teaching Roles
    Teaching and teaching excellence,
    State of the art knowledge on the subject,
    Expertise in pedagogical tools,
    Facilitation of student learning
Service
    Perform as assigned,
    Citizenship and contribution to the department,
    Participate in department and school meetings,

Keep informed
Collegial
TP rights and responsibilities were also defined.
　　Executive Committee: No
　　Senior Staff Committee: Yes
　　Academic Promotion and Tenure Committee: No.
　　MBA Oversight Committee: Yes
　　MS Oversight Committee: Yes
　　PhD Oversight Committee: No
　　Undergraduate Oversight Committee: Yes
　　Teaching Enhancement Committee: Yes
　　Merit Pay Review Committee: Yes, TP Subcommittee
　　Raise basis: 75% teaching quality, 25% service
　　Centers (including Director): Yes
　　Faculty Council: Yes
　　Participation in but not chair a dissertation committee
　　Eligible for all teaching awards
　　No differentiation in office space, department governance
　　Normally three year contract with one-year notice

The committee presented its report at a monthly school-wide assembly. A draft revised Constitution was also circulated with the indication that there would be a vote on the changes at the next monthly assembly.

A month passed. One hour before our assembly, I received a telephone call from an associate provost. I was forbidden to bring the constitutional change up for a vote.

I am quite liberal in my interpretation of academic policies and feel free to act when there is no policy restricting me. I do not violate direct orders. If I couldn't bring the constitutional change for a vote, what could I do? I decided to propose that the school adopt an "operating policy" document. It would start out the same as the constitution but would evolve to include major changes. And, since it was not a constitution, it wouldn't need two-thirds approval or two meetings for changes, and changes would not need to be approved by the University Senate. In reality, this was a subterfuge to avoid appearing to violate university policy while actually doing so.

So I went to the assembly, related the conversation with the associate provost, and proposed the "operating policy" strategy. It was approved. We then debated the teaching professor proposal. It was adopted by about a 95% positive vote.

At my next monthly meeting with the provost, I complained about the cease and desist order to not vote on the new constitution. He responded that Teaching Professor was not an approved university title, the Senate wouldn't approve such a change, and "certain people" were complaining. He added, "You can't pass a constitution that won't be approved." This made no sense to me, and I decided to ignore the provost's words. (It was also clear that one or more of my faculty members were reporting on our actions to the provost. While I considered this dirty pool, I didn't pursue it.)

A year later, the provost raised the TP title topic and told me again that certain people in the Senate were again complaining. I again ignored him.

Another year passed. This time, the provost stated that we had to stop using the TP title. I asked what our alternative was and was told that we would have to formally submit a request for the Senate to approve the position title. The request should specify why we needed the title, alternatives to the title, and what other universities were using the title. Ideally I should also get letters of support from the other university colleges.

I replied that we would prepare a proposal and after months of research, submitted the proposal to the Senate. About six weeks later, we received a list of questions about our proposal. We were nearing the end of the academic year. I decided that we could buy another year if we didn't respond until then.

Our new proposal was submitted in the next academic year. It was rejected. I was again ordered to stop using the TP title. Having no alternative, we changed the name. The new name would be "Teaching Fellow," another unapproved title. To short cut possible objections to this title, we decided to make this an honorary title, awarded to teachers of exemplary teaching. The full title would be "Tyser Teaching Fellow," named after a graduate of the school who had established an endowment fund to enhance teaching. Each Tyser Teaching Fellow would receive a small award from this endowment in recognition of their performance.

We built a cadre of TPs of 15–20 wonderful teachers and colleagues. We reduced our dependence on an army of adjuncts. Loads on the tenure track faculty were lower because of the TPs. The overall quality of our teaching improved. Everything but the name had been a spectacular success.

Organizing for Effectiveness

We conducted an extensive review of existing units and operations with the aim of streamlining operations. I worked with one center trying to craft a plan for the center that would be aligned with the school's strategy. After nine months, I gave up and decided to either close it down or transfer it to another part of the university. This move was not without pain, as the director of the center had a strong constituency and acted as if he, not I, was dean. During one confrontation in my office (which was on the second floor), that director volunteered that the previous dean had threatened to "throw him out of the window." My response was: "I wouldn't do that. It's not high enough. I would take you up to the roof and throw you off."

We also had a battle over that center's fund balances in the university foundation. The center had accumulated over $400,000 in cash while the business school had been paying its staff and not charging it rent or charging for services to the center. I won the battle and kept the money although I suspect that the provost gave them some back from his own funds.

We also transferred a large state contract to provide small business services. The contract was a loser. We were not properly compensated for our work and did not have the staff to do the work. When I asked the contract director why we had taken the contract, I was told that the president forced them to do it. This sounded rather strange to me, but I didn't spend any time trying to learn the facts.

I found that there was little financial management in the school. Administrative support was scattered among the academic departments and administrative units but there were no standards or coordination anywhere in the school.

It was impossible to manage the school under this structure. It took me about two years to fire the existing financial support staff and restructure the financial operations into a central operation reporting to the dean.

The administrative support units of the school were similarly restructured and the school's Office of Executive Programs redesigned. The administrative and finance organization was now headed by the former chief operating officer of a commercial organization and an entirely new staff had been put in place.

The management of the Office of Executive Programs was changed and a former senior manager from the Wharton School hired to run the office. A new staff was recruited, and new programs, including an EMBA, were launched.

During the summer before I became dean, I collected all of the literature published by the school. Many of the individual pieces were reasonable, but collectively, the school's literature was a mess. There was no coherence, no overall message, no graphic identity, and little sense in what was being produced.

The cause of this mess was obvious to me. Literature and brochures were being designed and produced by well meaning but untalented amateurs scattered across the school. One of my first mandates was that all new brochures and publicity pieces had to be approved by the dean's office. A second step was to create a single school-wide marketing communications department, headed by an assistant dean hired from the commercial world.

Within two to three years, I transformed the school from a decentralized operation managed by amateurs to a centralized system of professional managers. Senior administration now included the dean, a senior associate dean, two associate deans, and five assistant deans, with responsibilities ranging from development and marketing communications to management of the academic and career management programs. There were also six department chairs; eight center directors and co-directors; and faculty directors for research, master's programs, and other special programs. There were also several faculty committees that focused on teaching enhancement and undergraduate, master's, and Ph.D. programs.

It took years, but slowly our management went from poor to mediocre to good to excellent.

Chapter 5

Change Comes from Without

Advisory Council and Board

I inherited an advisory group of alumni and executives called "The Dean's Advisory Council." Members included friends of the last two deans and some older alumni. I had no idea what to do with the group. Some of the council were very well meaning and wanted to help me. Others hadn't attended meetings in years.

I didn't do much with the group for the first two or three years other than to hold two meetings each year where we briefed the council about the school's programs. We did, however, adopt term limits for membership and in this way began to drop inactive members from the group and to bring potential supporters and donors into the group. The council slowly became more active. It adopted several projects, such as student mentoring. Members began to donate to the school.

Efforts accelerated after a new assistant dean of development joined my staff. She proposed that we create a second board, a "Board of Visitors." The Board of Visitors would be made up of executives, while membership in the Council of Advisors would be restricted to alumni. The Board would be oriented towards partnerships with corporations, student placement, and marketing and branding. The Council would have student mentoring, funds raising, and building an alumni network.

Each group would have a committee structure. The chair of the Council would also be a member of the Board of Visitors.

The groups would become vehicles to develop friends and supporters of the school. If we encountered a prominent alumnus who was interested in becoming involved, we would invite him or her to join the Council. If we met a senior business executive who could recruit out students, we might offer membership in the Board.

Each group expanded to 30–40 individuals. They began to suggest projects for the school. For example, the Council of Advisors proposed that we lease a suite at the basketball arena. They then raised the money to make this happen. The suite would be an effective way of bringing recruiters, executives, and other potential supporters to meet with us. As I explained, "If I wanted to meet an executive, it might take me 2–3 months to schedule a meeting and a half day to travel to meet with him. I would then thank the executive for his time. With the suite, I could invite the individual to attend a basketball game. He would travel to us, I would spend some time with him during breaks, and he would thank me at the end of the game."

Ironically, the school's lease of a basketball suite became a source of contention with the university's administration. The lease had been working its way through university purchasing when suddenly the provost killed the deal. This would be especially damaging because our Council had already raised much of the money needed for the lease and many alumni had made commitments. If the provost's decision were not reversed, it would be, at best, very embarrassing but also very confusing because the president and other university operations had similar suites.

I went to the provost's office ready to do battle. In my suit pocket was my letter of resignation. I loved my job and didn't want to resign, but if the provost did not reverse his decision, I would be forced to, because if I allowed him to micromanage me in this area, what else might he do? In the end, the provost did reverse himself. He couldn't explain, other than to say, "it might not look good," why they didn't want us to have a suite. I agreed that no state money would be used to pay for the lease. And I personally would have to guarantee the debt.

Marketing: Getting the Word Out

I believe in marketing and promotion. I've seen how a small operation can gain a large footprint by aggressively promoting itself. Even
though I had no idea how to promote a business school, I decided
that anything would be better than nothing, so I created our first
promotional strategy.

Each month, we would place three pieces of mail on the desk of
every business school dean. Two would be simple "announcement"
cards notifying deans about new hires, promotions, events, and the
like. My goal for these was to have the dean see the name Smith. The
third would be a more substantive document such as a brochure, a
news article, or the description of a new program. Many of these
would promote our technology strategy.

We inaugurated the program with a letter to the deans describing
our technology strategy. Within three years, we were being ranked in
the top ten in information technology in surveys of business school
deans. Many deans remarked to me about Smith's promotional campaign, and some asked for details so they could emulate it.

Little by little we developed a comprehensive strategy to market
the school. I recruited an assistant dean for communications to lead
the effort. The communications group staff grew from a single person
to a six-person team, and the communications budget tripled over a
four-year period (to about $1 million per year). It ultimately stabilized
at about $2 million per year. By "branding" the school as an innovator
in joining technology with business education, the Smith School of
Business differentiated itself from the competition. This created an
immediate image for the school, and all marketing communications
were integrated to deliver that message. Everything from department
and school brochures to the school's website to marketing themes
were redesigned to have a common "look-and-feel" to support this
message.

A variety of direct mail, advertising, and public relations programs
were used to promote the expansion of the part-time programs and
to increase name recognition—regionally, nationally, and with deans

and MBA and undergraduate program directors from other business schools. Not only did enrollment increase, but recognition-based rankings rose as well. For example, the *U. S. News and World Report* ranking of the part-time MBA jumped from twenty-two to the top fifteen, and its estimation of undergraduate education at Smith jumped from twenty-two to eighteen. Both ranking systems are based solely on reputation.

Regionally, the school became highly regarded, with frequent press coverage and rapidly increasing regional student applications for all of its programs. Further, virtually every major national or international survey now placed Maryland in the top ten in the technology categories of supply chain, e-commerce, information technology, and information systems, and there were frequent top twenty-five rankings for most of the school's academic departments. And, before *Computer World's* decision to discontinue its numerical ranking of the top twenty-five programs, the School rose from being unlisted (1996) to third on the list (1999).

Leaders for the Digital Economy

Our efforts at branding the Smith School as a technological leader took a major step when in 2002, we adopted the tag line "Leaders for the Digital Economy," which was first proposed by the chair of the marketing department. We conducted a variety of studies to test the value of the brand. We compared the tag lines from other business schools. We surveyed students, faculty, and alumni. We presented the tag line to my two advisory executive groups, the Board of Visitors and the Dean's Advisory Council.

In each case, the feedback was mixed. Some loved the tagline, but others hated it. I believed that their reactions were similar to their view of the technology strategy itself. Some were enthusiastic about the strategy, but others never got it.

Against the advice of a number of our supporters, I decided to adopt the brand. We rolled out the brand in the following months.

Our website, brochures, marketing campaigns, and recruiting efforts began to feature the "Leaders" tagline. There was no ambiguity in our message even though the feedback had been very ambiguous. The campaign had an immediate casualty. The former dean, an executive in the financial industry and a prominent member of my Board of Visitors, resigned from the Board. A number of other Board members were unhappy but did not leave. A year later, several of them approached me after viewing a DVD prepared by my communications department to present the Leaders concept in the context of education at Smith. "You were right," they told me. "It is a good brand."

I will never be sure that we picked the right tagline. As time went on, the impact of technology on business became even more obvious, and the tagline seemed to be less effective. Also, as the Smith School became more powerful, with international operations and strong entrepreneurial activities, the tagline became dated. We dropped it in favor of a broader set of concepts:

- Technology
- Globalization
- Entrepreneurship

To make these words more than just marketing talk, we revised the offerings of our MBA programs to include required courses in each of these areas and created a series of technology, globalization, and entrepreneurship electives.

Facilities Again

The business school is housed in a modern facility, Van Munching Hall, first built and occupied in the early 1990s. Within a few years, the building proved far too small for the school. Faculty found themselves teaching undergraduate courses in as many as seventeen buildings on campus in any given year. In addition, the school ran out of office space, and while every faculty member had a private office, many other functions were crammed into tight and inadequate spaces. There was little room for visitors or adjuncts. Corporate recruiters were forced into tiny interview spaces. Numerous Ph.D. students were packed into bullpens. To make matters worse, the university's long-range facilities master plan provided for no additional business school facilities through 2015.

Correcting the facilities problems by getting additional space became a goal. Having enough classrooms in the school for all of our students was my highest priority. In the summer of 2002, the school took occupancy of a new 103,000 square foot wing of Van Munching Hall. This made a big impact on our classroom shortage, but the additional rooms still weren't enough.

In 2006 I concluded that we would need to build another wing of about 40,000 square feet. I enlisted Bob Smith's help, and he committed $3 million for the project. I then went to the provost and president to get their support. The president told me that he would support the project but "no matter what it costs, the university won't pay a penny." And I couldn't borrow because loans would impact the university's total debt limit.

I would need all cash. I agreed, the Board of Regents approved the project, and I secured a $6 million commitment from the state. My trip to Singapore and China with the governor had paid dividends.

Even though we didn't have the remainder of the money (estimated to be another $10 million), we commissioned architects for design and then issued a formal procurement. This needed to be approved by the state's Board of Public Works, but if I used private (non-state) money for the initial work, I could begin development before approval.

Within a year, we had raised the required money. One Smith graduate committed $2.5 million, another $1.5 million, and a third $1 million. Many others donated hundreds of thousands of dollars. The new (North) wing was completed in 2008, and when the final bill came due, we had the cash to pay for it.

We had reached our goal. All of our College Park classes could now be held within our building.

Dealing with Faculty

Professors are a mixed lot. Some are mature, public minded adults who are willing to sacrifice personal goals for the greater good. Others are like children—selfish and self centered. Those in the first group are a pleasure to work with. Many of my department chairs were in this group. Some selflessly built their departments in spite of their desires to spend more time on research. All of my senior associate deans were strong team players. This was not surprising because I picked team players to be my deputies.

There were many professors who would step up to help the school. One associate professor of marketing rolled up his sleeves to manage a group selling MBA projects. Another volunteered to develop an "assessment" program for the school. Several volunteered to be chairs of our various committees. Our teaching professors were extraordinary contributors with TP after TP assuming leadership roles in the school.

Individuals in the selfish group are a pain and rarely stay with the school no matter what you do for them.

During my eleven years as dean, I lost track of the number of requests and demands for salary increases. One professor complained annually no matter what his raise. He refused to accept salary surveys that showed he was one of the highest paid professors in his field and told others that I didn't like him and was out to get him.

Another was in my office all the time, asking for special consideration and special treatment. This young assistant and then associate professor was a terrific teacher and researcher, so I did everything I could to accommodate him. He ultimately left for a higher salary and a full professorship at a third rate university.

A third professor, also a fine teacher and researcher, would nickel and dime us for additional salary and special benefits. One day I received an e-mail from a researcher in another country questioning the originality of a section in one of the professor's papers. I asked my senior associate dean to investigate. He concluded that there was evidence of plagiarism, and we initiated a formal inquiry. The professor left the school before the inquiry was complete.

One full professor, a wonderful teacher and able researcher, appeared to me to have an inferiority complex. Every month or two, he would have to give me a detailed briefing about what he was doing, what he had done, and what he would do. He was always positioning for a larger raise than he might otherwise receive. His major shortcoming was that he was a lousy record keeper and was always late in submitting expense reports. Therefore, he was always asking for exceptions to policy. Because he was a valuable contributor to the school, I frequently complied.

A succession of faculty requesting special deals haunted my office. The department chairs were often not the most decision-oriented managers. Having come from the faculty and knowing that they would be returning to the faculty in a few years, they were reluctant to be very firm. Instead, knowing that there was a tougher guy in the dean's office, the chairs would send the faculty to me. In nearly all cases I rejected the requests, which included course reductions, more summer research money, or higher salaries.

The most unusual case involving a professor occurred early in my deanship. A few months after I came to Maryland, a professor approached me during a public meeting and asked me why I hadn't met with him. Not knowing why he had slipped through the cracks, I told my assistant to schedule a meeting immediately. She said she would and rolled her eyes. "We were trying to keep him away from you," she told me.

I asked my senior associate dean about the faculty member, and her response was simple, "Oh him, he's crazy."

The next day, I met with the man. My curiosity turned to alarm as he described plots by students and faculty against him. His office door had been glued shut. Students were out to get him. There were spies in the school. "People would like to see me floating face up in the Potomac," he told me confidentially. The meeting ended, and

I demanded a full briefing about him. After I received it, I became even more alarmed. Some time ago, he had been normal—a good colleague, teacher, and promising researcher. Then something had happened, and the man had changed. He was now paranoid. He no longer did research and was a terrible teacher. His teaching ratings were horrendous and his relations with people bizarre.

Previous deans had ignored the problem. They had inflicted him on our undergraduates. I could not. At the end of the semester, I removed him from the classroom, gave him an assignment that he could perform at home, and sent him there. We also alerted his psychiatrist to our actions. He never returned to the school and a few years later took early retirement.

Another early problem was a professor whom I discovered was teaching one half of the normal course load per year. This professor, an economist with an international reputation, reported that a previous dean had reduced his workload. Naturally, there was nothing in writing and no recollection of the "deal" by anyone else. Year after year, department chairs honored the phantom deal and the dean's office did nothing to interfere.

I told the professor that this situation could not continue. He would have a normal course load in the next academic year. The professor filed a personnel action against me with the university. The provost confirmed that I had the authority to change course loads. The professor and I spent the next few months debating his course load, when the dispute suddenly ended. The professor had a heart attack while working out and died. It's a tough way to end an argument. He was a nice man.

Another death occurred when a fine individual committed suicide. I was asked to preside over a memorial service for him in the university chapel. I had never done anything like this before, and I hope I never have to do it again.

The chair of one of my departments approached me about a full professor who was two years from retirement. The chair complained that the professor was a poor teacher, a poor researcher, and a poor colleague. He asked me to remove the professor from the department.

I asked the provost to approve an "early termination package" for the professor. I offered the professor full salary to leave the school a year early. The professor accepted, and I thought the problem was solved.

A year later I learned that the professor's former department had voted to elect the professor to "emeritus" status. Academics are often conflict adverse and had voted unanimously for the appointment. I told the department chair that I would oppose the action. (Emeritus is an honorary appointment conferred upon distinguished retired faculty, requiring university approval.) Nevertheless, the department referred the election to the entire faculty for a vote. It was again unanimous. The action then was on my desk for transmittal to the university's promotion and tenure committee. Given the department's opinions regarding the professor's contributions, I could not agree to the appointment and so opposed it in a letter to the provost. The university concurred with my position and the emeritus status was denied. Following this action, the professor called me, yelled at me, and finished with the parting statement: "This job has changed you. You used to be a nice guy." He then hung up. I was about to respond, "You're wrong. I've never been a nice guy. It's a façade," but before I could speak, the phone was dead.

In spite of the many negative interactions with faculty, my feelings towards faculty were very positive; I had many rewarding relationships. I met one finance professor during my initial get acquainted meetings. We spent time discussing my technology and business strategy. He didn't get it, so I invited him back to continue discussions. Two meetings later he brought a document he had written about how technology impacts finance. It was an exciting work. He did get it! Later that year, he came to me with a proposal to build a financial trading center in the school. Five major business schools had such trading centers, which could be an excellent competitive edge.

I told him that it was a great idea. The way to proceed, I suggested, was to get the finance department to propose the idea in their next strategic plan but not to mention that he had discussed the concept with me. A few months later the finance department presented me with a plan to build a financial trading center. The plan included additional hiring, funding, and space requirements. I complimented the department on the plan, gave them my full support, and told them I would find the money and space.

The center was in operation within a year. Three years later, we opened a second center with more than twice the space.

Another faculty member, a full professor, brought me the resume of a supply chain expert who had been working with him on research projects. The professor recommended that we find a way to hire him. The individual looked terrific and fit perfectly with the technology strategy, so I pieced together three sources of funding to hire him. The man became a research professor and a very supportive colleague.

Tenure

The major milestone for a young faculty member is to receive tenure. The tenure system is very demanding. A new assistant professor has seven years to develop a record of research and teaching worthy of tenure. If the professor is granted tenure, he is promoted to associate professor. If he or she is not granted tenure, the professor has one more year of employment at the school and then must leave.

It is expected that an assistant professor's progress will be reviewed in the third year to gauge the prospect of tenure and the professor's accomplishments to date. If the professor has not made satisfactory progress towards tenure, that professor can be given more time or can be asked to leave after the fourth year.

When I first became dean, the school had a very rigorous tenure review system but erratic three-year reviews. I began to stress that the three-year review system should be more demanding. Professors who had little prospect of tenure should be asked to leave. Letting them stay around was very costly to the school in both dollars and opportunity costs. If a weak professor left, we could replace the individual with one with better prospects. Also, it wasn't fair to the individual to have them stay seven or eight years at Maryland when they could be investing their time at an institution where they would have better chances. Within a few years, our three-year reviews became much more substantive, with several faculty being asked to leave.

The tenure process worked in the following way. First a department committee reviewed the professor's record. As part of the review, they solicited letters from leading academics at other institutions to comment on their research. A dossier would be prepared, and the department would vote on the case. Negative votes could be very damning. The next step would be for the entire tenured faculty to review the tenure case. Another vote would then be held, with the results reported to me.

I would then review the case and the results of the votes. I would prepare a detailed letter for submission to the provost and the university's tenure committee. In my letter I would have to explain the reasons for negative votes (if any) as well as any negative comments that might appear in the external letters of recommendation. Negative comments and votes would again be very damning.

My recommendation, while not sufficient to bestow tenure, would have great weight if it were negative. Indeed, it was unlikely that tenure would be granted if the dean was against it. Also, once or twice each year, I would be asked to attend a university tenure committee meeting to answer explicit questions about a faculty member's record. I usually took the department chair with me to such meetings because the chair had much better knowledge of the professor than I did.

In my first ten years as dean I never lost a tenure case, and twice I took the opposite position from the faculty, with my recommendation being approved. In the eleventh year, the university committee and/or the provost and president gave me a lot of problems. It nearly felt like they wanted to teach me a lesson. I will never know.

Chapter 6

Growing Pains

Long Range Strategic Goals

The continuing strategy of the school was to provide focus and drive from the dean's office in a constant effort to expand the school along the lines of its strategy. Creating an environment where the vision comes from the top, but bottom-up innovation is encouraged, is perhaps the key to the school's success. There's no way that a single individual, no matter how talented, can build a major academic enterprise.

Top leadership of the school, while outlining a distinct vision, would not micro-manage every aspect of implementing the vision. Providing faculty members and staff with the freedom and resources to define, extend, and implement the vision in their own areas of specialization generated many new ideas. For example, all of the school's new centers and laboratories have been faculty or department-proposed concepts. I was involved in selecting, prioritizing, and finding funding for new initiatives. The process typically proceeded as follows: one (or a few) faculty proposed an initiative. They tested the idea for feasibility with their department chairs and the dean's office. Next, they gained support in their department to make their initiative a part of the department's strategic plan. The department plan was then integrated into the school-wide plan and incorporated into the school's budget and five-year financial forecast.

To illustrate, the school created a behavioral research laboratory, proposed by faculty a year earlier, and the Center for Entrepreneurship closed a $20 million venture capital fund, first proposed by that Center's director and staff.

As to the future of the Robert H. Smith School of Business, I believe that the school will continue to expand and articulate its vision. The school's status in the national rankings will continue to rise, with the goal of housing a top fifteen MBA program, a top ten undergraduate experience, and a top ten Ph.D. program as measured by a combination of external rankings and criteria such as research, placement, and teaching quality.

At least four of the school's academic departments will be among the top fifteen in research in the country; and overall, the school will rank among the top five in research. The end result will manifest itself in student job placements and salaries at or above those of graduates from Smith's peer institutions. The School will have a dominant regional position in a broad family of programs and activities and will have national recognition through outreach efforts geared towards executive and management development and entrepreneurship. Finally, state-of-the-art physical and technology facilities will continue to add to Smith's attraction and continue to offer the technical capabilities that support the School's agenda.

Raising Money

Deans are expected to spend significant time raising money. The dean is the chief fund-raiser and is expected to be the "closer" for major gifts. In my earlier experiences as CEO for three companies, I had become adept at generating business. I had made many sales of intangible consulting and software projects and had become an effective practitioner of the "consultative" sale, where you find out what a company needs, craft and propose a solution to meet those needs, and then close the sale.

These experiences didn't prepare me fully for the "psychic" sale, where the potential donor has no tangible need to fill. My first major proposal was rather silly. The target was an aging donor who had been a successful real estate developer. I visited him without much preparation. Soon after our initial handshake, he asked me why I was there. I responded, "I would like you to donate $1.5 million to the business school." To the gentleman's credit, he continued the meeting. He was polite but firm in rejecting the proposal. He asked me to call him in a few months. I did but was asked to call again. After three or four such exchanges, I stopped calling.

My second effort had a different middle game but the same outcome. Again the prospect was a successful real estate developer. This fellow was delighted to see me. He invited me to lunch and we talked about his business and the business school. Lunch was repeated several times until I began talking about a donation to the school. His response was: "What has the university ever done for me?" Even though we developed a very friendly relationship, we never received a dime.

My assistant dean for development told me she had a major contributor ready to make a million dollar gift to the school. To close the deal, both the president and I would have to visit. Unfortunately, he was based in Chicago and we would have to travel there during miserable winter weather. We both made it and spent a very frustrating hour, finally walking away without a commitment. I was both annoyed and embarrassed. It was a waste of my time, but we had dragged the president there too.

I must have closed several small donations because my first semester wasn't all bleak. Then, Bob Smith made his naming gift to the business school and I became a fund-raising hero. This bought me the time to do the right things.

We had to build our development staff. Having a single development person was absurd. Other schools had fifteen, twenty, or even thirty staff. Our tiny operation was an elegant example of the university's myopic vision. Development was a centrally funded and managed operation, with the schools' development officers reporting to the deans on a "dotted line" basis. Within two to three years I expanded the development staff to five people, with the goal of building it to a ten-person organization. I paid for the additional people from business school funds. When we reached ten people, my target became twenty people.

The split reporting arrangements frequently caused stress. My management style was very different than that of the VP for university advancement. I believe in hiring excellent people, paying them well, giving them direction, and then letting them perform. This was not the way university advancement was managed. Consequently I had many arguments about my staffs' salaries. Because I didn't have the final say, my staff was underpaid and had high turnover.

We had to do many things. We had to build a pipeline of prospects. You may need ten prospects to close one deal. We needed clean data about our alumni. The university couldn't supply this, so we had to generate it ourselves.

You don't just ask people for money. You find ways to engage them in the life of the school. Then, after they are sufficiently committed, you ask them to help in areas that have special meaning to them. Having been students themselves, most potential donors like to help students. Therefore we worked to create an alumni mentor network. The effort took several years, but its result was hundreds of alumni working with students. Many of these made donations to the school.

Significant donations began to take place. I closed several exceeding one million each. I developed the following approach. I would first meet the prospect and tell him what was happening at the Smith School. I might then invite him or her to visit us at the school. After a tour of our facilities, I would introduce the prospect to students and some of our staff. I might ask him to join one of our advisory boards. One of the first questions I was asked was usually, "What do you want from me? Do you want a donation?" My response was nearly always a variation of, "I don't know you well enough to ask you for anything. If I did ask you for money, you might give us some, but it would probably be 'go away' money and not enough."

We raised $29 million in my first five years as dean. We raised another $90 million in the next six years.

Mobilizing the Alumni

Strong alumni support for a university and its colleges is critical. Alumni donate money. They help students get jobs. They interview perspective students and recommend the schools' programs. They add to the reputation of the schools. I'd like to say that I found a strong alumni network, but this was hardly the case. What I found was another mess.

My first experience with alumni took place when I was invited to attend an alumni reception in New York. My wife and I decided to spend the weekend in the city. When the taxi dropped us off at the reception's location, we weren't sure we were in the right place. It was in a seedy building in a seedy area of lower Manhattan. The second floor reception area was hardly better. I returned home and sent a critical e-mail to the university's vice president of development, copying our new president, who had joined us a month earlier. It was clear from the V.P.'s response that he didn't "get it." (A few months later, he was fired. Our new president did get it.)

Alumni relations in the business school were no better. We shared an alumni director with the University Office of Alumni Relations. The director didn't report to me, and there was no budget for the position. With no resources, nothing was being done. Our alumni were never contacted. It was as if once they graduated, they had never existed.

Engagement and integration of the alumni into a powerful support network for the school would be the school's greatest challenge. The university and the business school started late in cultivating alumni. The University's Alumni Association was not founded until 1988. Building an alumni network would be a multi-year process. It would take both marketing and promotion and many additional dollars. I discussed this problem with the new Vice President of Advancement, but I could never get any additional money. I decided that if Smith were to become the powerhouse that I envisioned, we would have to do it ourselves.

We began the process by transforming a rather mediocre newsletter into a full-fledged, handsome magazine. We sent the magazine to every graduate with an address in the university's database. Getting correct addresses was itself a monumental problem because the database was poorly maintained. We also began building an Office of External Relations. Over the course of my tenure, the office grew from one person to more than twenty.

One activity was event management. As our commitment to external relations grew, so did the number of receptions, seminars, lunches, dinners, and other meetings. At the start, the sponsors of the meeting were responsible for organizing and managing administrative aspects such as registration, catering, and facilities management. Some meetings were managed well but others were mismanaged because the sponsors were amateurs. To deal with this problem, I centralized management of important events within the Event Management Group. They did a terrific job with a few dedicated people, and we went from being able to manage meetings with a few dozen people to ones with hundreds of attendees.

Today, 30,000 active members of Smith's alumni association mentor current students through an organized program of professional shadowing and ongoing communication. They participate in an online network whose goal is to maximize the value of the Smith School experience by enabling students to interact with alums in discussion groups and other networking events. They run leadership programs for our freshmen and participate in the life of the school. The job, however, is not complete. It will be another decade before alumni are fully engaged.

The Foundation

The business school had a private foundation operating as a 501C3 corporation for the benefit of the school. It was managed as an arms-length corporation with a separate board of directors. The foundation was a source of considerable antagonism from the university administration because we were the only school with such an entity. I don't know how or why it originally was established, but because of the university's bureaucracy, it gave the school flexibility that other schools didn't have. It also generated hostility and jealousy because most people thought the foundation had many millions of dollars of assets. It didn't. It had a tiny annual budget, and its principal activities were supporting an MBA student investment fund with about $800,000 of assets and being the financial agent for our Executive Programs Office.

Before I arrived, the school had infuriated the university by giving small (about $5,000 each) payments from the foundation to two assistants in the business school, contravening university human resources procedures. I was told this was to compensate them for administrative work for the foundation. In spite of the complaints about the foundation, it was a valuable resource. Because the university's billing and collection procedures were inept, we ran executive education through the foundation. Therefore, the foundation's financial base expanded as our executive education revenues expanded, and it began to accumulate assets.

When the managers of our entrepreneurship center (named the Dingman Center for Entrepreneurship) came to me with a proposal to start a venture capital fund, I was an enthusiastic supporter. The center wrote a proposal to the US Small Business Administration (SBA) for matching funds. The proposal was the highest ranked proposal of the year, and the fund was awarded a $10 million loan. To secure the loan, the fund would have to raise $10 million of equity from investors.

The successful proposal had the following differentiating concepts:

* Invest in underprivileged areas,
* Assist companies with marketing, technical, and business issues through student advisors and consulting grants,
* Use MBA and engineering students as program managers,
* Operate within the business school facility,
* Teach a venture capital course to students.

In addition to the $10 million loan, the fund was awarded a $3 million matching grant for consulting assistance. Again the fund would have to raise $3 million to receive the match. The business school foundation was a prospective investor. The foundation board evaluated the proposal and decided to invest $500,000.

Quite independent of the foundation's investment decision, the university insisted on greater and greater controls over the foundation's activities. They insisted that an individual from the university approve every check that the foundation would write. (Whether or not the university had the legal authority to impose this control was never resolved because the university refused to address the concerns of the foundation's president as expressed in a letter to the president of the university.) As an officer of the university, I was duty bound to follow the university's directions, even though I thought them heavy-handed and misguided.

Even though the foundation board had approved the investment and committed to an initial $50,000 capital call, the new requirement was a stumbling block because the individual put in charge insisted on answers to a series of questions that I considered outside of his scope. The issue came to a head when the foundation made a $50,000 wire transfer. We received a scathing e-mail from the vice president of university advancement. I was furious and responded with this letter and e-mail (I've changed names):

Re: Oversight of Robert H. Smith School of Business Foundation

This memo is in response to your January 17, 2003 memo. It's unfortunate that you wrote your memo without calling me first to discuss the topic because your letter has factual misstatements, serious errors of omission and is personally insulting. We have exhibited complete candor and openness at the regular weekly reviews with Mr. Jack. To state that a serious violation occurred is unfair and irresponsible.

On December 13, 2002, the Smith Foundation received notification of the SBA's final sign-off of the New Markets Growth Fund. As part of this sign-off, all papers were required to be signed and returned to the New Markets Growth Fund no later than December 18, 2002, with the initial capital call due on January 7, 2003. It was during this time that Mr. Jack expressed concern about the investment. The President of the Foundation and another Board member then spoke with Jack. Mr. Jack understood the need to sign the Board approved subscription agreement. Further, Mr. Jack was informed that the Board was also requesting a written legal opinion before the next capital call. On December 23, 2002, the Smith Foundation received notification that the first capital call deadline had been extended to January 10, 2003 due to the holidays. The wire transfer could have been made before December 31st, but was made on January 9, 2003 to best manage the Foundation cash.

The signing of the subscription agreement required the Smith Foundation to meet its financial commitment. If we had not honored the capital call, the $20,000,000 Venture Capital Fund closing would have been seriously impaired, a very damaging impact on the Business School and the University.

In addressing Mr. Jack's concerns about the Fund, we requested and received verbal assurance from the law firm that the arrangements are in compliance with State conflict rules. We also requested a written opinion to this effect (see attached memo) [not included here]. Mr. Jack received a copy of this memo on January 3rd.

The initial capital commitment of $50,000 is part of a $500,000 investment of the Smith Foundation in the New Markets Venture Fund. The Smith Foundation Board reviewed this investment for over one year. Substantial due diligence was conducted on this investment to determine if it was appropriate for the Foundation in terms of the Foundation's purpose and investment criteria. The Board on March 5, 2002, unanimously approved the investment in the New Market Growth Fund.

Campus has been aware from the outset that this was a project that the Dingman Center was pursuing. At the outset of this activity,

Dr. Ronald Spiral and I met with the president to understand his concerns and to make sure that our approach was consistent with University policy. As a matter of fact, the president was present with Senator Sarbanes in May 2002 when the Federal Home Loan Bank Board presented the Dingman Center with a check for $250,000 for the Fund. At all times, we have conducted our activities with full knowledge of the University and have continuously kept the president and the provost apprised of the progress of the New Markets Venture Fund.

While the Smith Foundation Board may appreciate an outside perspective on the Fund investment, the review and interpretation of the Fund was taken very seriously and with extreme care and fiduciary responsibility over a long period of time. For the Smith Foundation not to honor this financial commitment at this time because of some concerns (a few days prior to closing) from an outsider with limited knowledge and facts would be less than prudent on the part of the Foundation. Further, the issues raised in your letter are not related to the Smith Foundation's investment but rather Business School operations and activities. They go beyond either yours or Mr. Jack's authorities. Also, Mr. Jack is not an officer of the Smith Foundation and has no legal authority to sign checks.

Finally, I find receiving and writing letters like this to be offensive and should I continue to receive them, I will act appropriately.

My letter did not close the issue. I received another from the same vice president.

I am glad to have received your e-mail/letter. I have little doubt that the arrangement between the Smith School Foundation and the New Markets Venture Fund is fair and square, though it is essential for Mr. Jack's questions to be addressed fully. The action that prompted, indeed required, my letter, was the uncontestable fact that, contrary to the explicit understanding between the College Park Foundation and the Smith School Foundation, a disbursement of $50,000 was made by the Smith School Foundation without prior review by the College Park Foundation's CFO. There is or there is not prior review. In this instance, there was not. Hence, we needed to take action to ensure that disbursements under the same conditions do not happen again.

I responded with another belligerent e-mail:

> You are just outright wrong. Mr. Jack was told that the disbursement was going to be made and that it needed to be made to meet the call notification. His comment was "I understand." If he had disapproved, he should have said so at the time, before the due date so the matter could have been dealt with, if necessary, on appeal to higher authorities.

The president's instruction in his letter of November 7 was that "the change does not unnecessarily impair Smith School operations and programs." To not make this payment would have been a serious blow to the Fund and seriously impaired an important program.

As I indicated in my letter, Mr. Jack's questions do not relate to the Foundation. They relate to the relationship between various parties in the business school and the New Markets Growth Fund. As far as I know, neither Mr. Jack nor you are in charge of the business school or in charge of academic affairs. To step in at the last moment and foul up such an important effort is simply unacceptable. It cannot continue.

Mr. Jack also has no authority to sign Smith Foundation checks and independent of what I might be willing to do, I have no authority to allow him to sign checks. This authority can only be granted by the Foundation's Board of Directors, which is a 501C3 corporation with legal corporate governance requirements.

Finally, this letter/e-mail process is very destructive. When you sent me your surprise letter on Friday, you placed a damaging and unjustified accusation on the record. I was forced to respond to set the record straight. I will not be conducting further correspondence regarding this matter.

We then discussed the issues raised by telephone. But the exchanges were now part of the record, with the provost and president being copied throughout the exchange.

Surrounded by Incompetence

I received the following memo from my senior associate dean:

> The Masters Program Office is having a terrible time with the various idiosyncratic billing arrangements with the students. The Bursar's Office is getting everything wrong, bills need to be constantly hand-checked, all 50 bills sent to the Baltimore students were wrong. Another person slipped through with tuition remission despite instructions to the contrary. Students are very frustrated and form poor impressions of the school.

The head of my Masters Program Office sent me a memo summarizing complaints for our students about the University's Financial Aid Office. A few extracts should suffice to give a picture of that office:

> "I found out after six months that my application was incomplete because no verification of my citizenship could be found. No one had mentioned this to me."
>
> "Every time I tried to connect to a representative, the voice mail says 'all circuits are busy' and returns me to the menu. After three times, I get a 'Good Bye' message and get disconnected."
>
> "I have recently gone through the process of applying for a student loan. It took me a while to find the right building on campus and the right office. When I reached it, I was given the wrong information and the wrong form."

In another memo, our international students detailed the problems of the International Education Services (IES). They detailed a series of poor policies, including stringent and inflexible requirements, user-unfriendly practices, dictatorial personnel, and excessive response times to student questions.

Every month I would participate in a "Deans' Council" meeting with the provost and all of the deans on campus. We would have periodic complaint sessions. The Procurement Department was the number one villain. It seemed that no one could get this department to work for them. As an example, I sent the provost the following:

> Procurement has turned into a nightmare. Nearly every day I hear about cases that would turn our hair gray (if both of us didn't have that color already.) Today I was told that Procurement is holding up payments to the Washington Post for our Part Time Program advertising because we didn't have sole source justifications and hadn't gone through a competitive procurement for the ads. Something needs to be done to get control of what is now a process out of control. (I also understand that the b-school isn't the only one being driven crazy. I'd be glad to come over to talk to you about this.)

The poor quality and high cost of campus dining was the second most hotly discussed subject. There appeared to be a campus policy mandating that everyone use Dining Services. No one could find anything in writing about this policy, but that didn't matter. Later, I would undertake a project to oust Dining Services as the business school's sole caterer.

The business school had a revenue sharing arrangement with the campus, but I couldn't get my forecasts to agree with the money we were getting from the campus. After complaining vigorously, they conducted an audit and found mistakes in their allocation processes.

I found that we were sending another school money for no understandable reason. When I finally found the right paperwork, it turned out that that other school should have been sending us money. I wrote a memo about my findings to the dean of the other school. In my memo, I pointed out that I wouldn't be sending them any more money, and that they owed us about $500,000, but I would forgive their debt. That dean complained to the provost, and I had to explain my actions to him. I never heard about the issue again except when the other dean would grumble something about our unfair action.

The university personnel office had many policies that made it more difficult to operate. It seemed that every time any school in the State of Maryland was caught doing something improper, the university added a policy to keep it from happening at our university. For example, because someone had once falsified their resume, new professors had to present signed resumes before they could be paid. A copy of a signed resume would not suffice. Payments were frequently delayed after a new assistant professor arrived on campus because we didn't have an original signed document.

Multiple copies of expense reimbursements had to be submitted and signed off. Many individuals and every expense required a receipt, no matter how small. The amount of paperwork was immense. The system operated as if everyone were a crook and the paperwork was the only way to keep them from stealing.

The university's controller and finance department insisted that we cast all of our finances in terms of our state budget and that every element of our state budget be balanced. They could not understand that for an operation in which the state budget was less than a third of total expenses, this was not possible. Nonetheless, we were forced to spend weeks recasting financials into meaningless forms.

The following speaks for itself. I received this e-mail from one of my staff. (I've changed names to protect the guilty):

> Here's the wire info............once you read this you'll know why taxes are what they are and why we try not to wire funds............
>
> The current PO (which expired June 30, 2007) only has $9K on it, so we're able to process only three invoices. Debra (campus A/P lady) needs to sign off on it and she's out sick, expected back on Friday, when she'll sign off and then send it to Judy (campus wire lady). By next Wednesday, we can ask Judy (campus wire lady) for the transaction information to pass to you for tracking..........

In the meantime, we've asked Brian (campus procurement guy) to increase the expired PO to cover the other invoices. He is out until Monday, but I don't anticipate any problem increasing this PO (since he's been working with us on the new PO)............once he increases the PO, it will go to Debra (campus A/P lady, who is presuming back from being sick) to sign off and then to Judy (campus wire lady, who hasn't gotten sick from campus A/P lady) to process. Then a few days later we can ask Judy (campus wire lady who is hopefully still with us) for the transaction information to pass to you for tracking...........

The $50K for the Business Plan Competition is on Brian's desk (campus Director of Procurement guy). This has now been put on a separate PO, so once Brian (campus Director of Procurement guy) signs off he will give to Debra (campus A/P lady, who was sick, but presuming is now back from being sick and hasn't become sick again because she came back to work too soon) to sign off, then to Judy (campus wire lady who is hopefully still with us, in spite of time passing and hasn't become sick from working with Debra—campus A/P lady) to process. Then a few days later we can ask Judy (campus wire lady who is hopefully still with us, in spite of time passing and hasn't become sick from working with Debra—campus A/P lady) for the transaction information to pass to you for tracking...........

So, if this summary hasn't made sense in terms of a timeline as to when you'll be receiving funds, now you know why we try not to wire funds.............and then try to track and confirm that they actually were processed...........

The university's undergraduate operation worked continuously to subvert the admittance policies that they had approved. The provost would admit unqualified students because he thought we were being too hard on them. Other deans and administrators would complain about our "elitism." We would be constantly pressured to teach more classes to non-business students even though I made it very clear that we didn't have the teaching capacity to do so. We had made an agreement to offer our undergraduate program at another campus at Shady Grove, Maryland. We agreed after the university offered us compensation for each student taught. We received a budget increase and were to get annual payments. The budget increase disappeared the very next year after a budget cut, and I had to fight for each annual payment, some of which never came.

While we were constantly working to keep too many undergraduate students from being admitted, the graduate school took inordinate amounts of time to admit qualified graduate students to our programs. They proved especially inept when it came to international students and international programs. Here's part of a memo I wrote to the provost complaining about this problem:

> The Smith School launched its first track of Executive MBA students in 2003 in Beijing at the University of International Business and Economics. About 60 students were in the first track. The second track, started in 2005, had 38 students and the current track, started in 2006, has less than 15 students. Smith launched an EMBA track in Shanghai in mid-2005 and is recruiting for another track in Shanghai. The school has not been able to enroll more than 20 students in Shanghai for its program despite the continued success of its major competitors.
>
> Admission cycles and TOEFL requirements have been major elements in the diminishing number of students. Flexibility in TOEFL requirements as well as MEI administered testing in China initially facilitated admissions. This is no longer the case. However, competitors such as the University of Southern California and INSEAD are able to admit students "on-the-spot" in China based on their academic records and oral interviews. It takes the Smith School 6–9 months to go through the University of Maryland's admissions process.

The school had a similar experience in Tunisia, where it began an Executive MS program in 2006. The school had more than 30 appropriate applicants but the Graduate School admitted fewer than twenty students. Many of these applications took 6–9 months to process.

Everywhere, in every place, we were surrounded by incompetence. There were some energetic, competent university staff, but the majority were lazy, unimaginative, and without initiative. When faced with an aggressive business school that would not accept the status quo, they were hostile and negative. We became the bad guys, and few outsiders had anything nice to say about my staff or me.

Campus Competition

The campus had a strange arrangement of its educational offerings. Courses offered during the summer and during the one-month "wintermester" between the fall and spring semesters were under a completely different management structure. They reported to a dean of continuing education. That office was also attempting to sell programs to corporate and government organizations.

The financial arrangements with this office were very one sided. Only about 20% of the profits were returned to the school teaching the courses. On observing this, I decided that the business school would not use precious faculty resources for 20% of the profit when we could teach courses off campus for 100% of the profits. Each year our summer school revenues decreased. One day, I received the following offensive e-mail from the provost in response to one of my continuing requests for more money:

> Your students are done a disservice by the failure of the Business School to offer summer courses, and this lack of offerings also negatively impacts our undergraduate retention and graduation rates. You complain about lack of

campus support, which is certainly debatable, but you refuse to take advantage of one of the largest revenue sources used by the colleges. Departments like computer science, for example, use adjunct faculty to teach their lower level summer school courses and they make out like a bandit.

I responded:
In other words, we should work harder to retain a benefit that we already have?
I do not have additional faculty to teach summer courses. We are stretched very thinly across our multiple part time MBA programs and these revenues are the only difference between total mediocrity and us.
How about giving us a more equitable base budget in line with the total number of credit hours we teach? (Sorry to put it so bluntly but I am becoming totally fed up with what I consider the inequitable treatment of the business school.)

And then sent him another e-mail to follow up.
I just noticed that in your e-mail, you refer to retention and graduation rates and that the business school is negatively impacting the university's rates. The data I have shows us with rates substantially exceeding the university's averages for four, five and six year graduation rates. Also, as you may know, we make every effort to provide sufficient course coverage to allow our students to graduate without taking summer courses. Finally, I've been led to believe that our retention and graduation rates are among the highest of all of the colleges so I'm wondering if your remark is more than just an offhand comment.

There was no response to my e-mails, but I subsequently learned that the provost received about 50% of the profits from summer school courses, so he had a built in incentive to get schools to teach in these programs. It must have really annoyed him that I was a profit-oriented manager and wouldn't play his game.

To make matters worse, the continuing education office was attempting to sell business education programs to corporations without our knowledge. They would recruit our faculty and pay them a stipend to teach in their programs in direct competition with us. We found that they were advertising completed projects on their website that actually had been done by the Smith School. At one point, they attempted to bid an executive business degree to a government agency. Fortunately, the provost caught this (he wasn't all bad) and sent it to me. I vetoed the proposal. I put a stop to this practice by prohibiting our faculty from teaching in their programs. Of course, I made another dean an enemy in the process. Later, the office was reorganized and their efforts to compete with other schools ceased.

A Fun Project

One of my favorite activities was working with Bob Smith. He was the school's true benefactor and I began calling him Saint Bob. He would visit the school every month or two to meet with me and to have lunch with a group of students, faculty, or staff. I would structure these lunches so that Bob would get in-depth briefings about one aspect of the school's activities. Lunches included meetings with endowed professors, new hires, assistant professors, PhD students, MBA students, undergraduate honors students, and the staffs of our various academic and administrative departments and centers. Each briefing would include a discussion of the group's current activities and strategic goals. Bob would conclude each lunch with a powerful statement of his support for the school. He would always ask me "How can I help?" I always had an answer.

After one lunch, we walked through the original Van Munching Hall, and I pointed out areas that had become shabby when compared to the new South Wing. Bob asked me to put together a plan to fix this.

A month later, we again walked through Van Munching Hall, this time with a list of refurbishments and changes. Back in my office, I gave him a list of the cost of the changes, totaling about $2 million.

The changes included elements like upgrading the technology in all original classrooms, upgrading lighting, new carpets and ceiling tiles, and painting the building. After each item on the list, Bob would volunteer to pay about one half of the cost, I would match his offer, and we would stand up and shake hands. By the end of the meeting, Bob had volunteered about $1 million and I had matched it with another $1 million, all at no cost to the university, which is responsible for facility management and maintenance. It was a fun day.

Thinking that I might offset part of the school's $1 million commitment, I submitted a proposal for classroom upgrades to the university. It was rejected.

We proceeded with the refurbishment. Each month, Bob and I would walk through the building and review the changes in progress. Six months later, we had completed the project at no cost to the university. It was another of the many examples where we had attempted to enlist the university's help, were turned down, and moved ahead on our own.

More Fun Stuff

Being dean was a heady experience. A large sign, "Welcome Dean Howard Frank," greeted me on entering Van Munching Hall on the first day of my deanship. My wife and I watched a football game from the President's Suite at the football stadium. The announcer broadcasted the same "Welcome Dean Howard Frank" message to the stadium. I was treated with deep respect wherever I went in the university.

I loved talking to students. I remember meeting with a group of students from our honors program. Our goal was to discuss ways to improve the program to make it more attractive to students. When they walked out of my office an hour later, I was elated. "I only wish," I said, "I could have as intelligent a conversation with my own children." It was at that moment that I decided I would stay as dean beyond my original five year commitment.

I am a sports fan. Maryland had a fine basketball team whose coach was a business school alumnus. (We won the national NCAA championship in 2002.) I invited him to be a guest at many of our alumni receptions, and one year he was keynote speaker at our graduation ceremonies. I reciprocated by attending numerous basketball games. The atmosphere was electric, the games were fine, and our guests were loyal supporters.

The university's athletic director sent me a chair from the floor of the Final Four in the year we won the NCAA basketball championship. I kept the chair in the most visible spot in the dean's office and would proudly point it out to new visitors.

We had a new football coach who turned around a mediocre team in his first year as coach. I met him several times and volunteered to assist in recruiting. By accident we met on a plane going from Washington to New York and spent an hour talking about his educational philosophy. This convinced me that he was genuinely interested in academics, and as a result, my associate dean and I crafted a plan to make the business school more receptive to student athletes. As I would say many times, "business and athletics are very much alike. You have to know how to pick yourself off the ground and get back into play. Student athletes who can complete our academic programs will make great business people."

The coach invited me to be on the sidelines during home football games. It's a fun but hard way to watch a game. You have to run up and down the sidelines to see plays, always taking care to not be run over by a fast moving TV camera vehicle. By halftime, I was exhausted and went home. (The fact that we were being annihilated on the field and it was pouring had something to do with my early exit.)

My wife and I also traveled with the team to North Carolina State, where our team pulled the game out in the last minutes of play. Neither of us (or any of the other Marylanders at the game) could speak after the game because we had cheered so loudly when we won. I was great fun and a reward for being dean.

The many parties, performances, banquets, dinners, and celebrations were entertaining. There were nice people, reasonable food, and good entertainment. At the beginning I attended every event because I wanted to demonstrate that I was involved in the life of the university. Individually, each was fun, but cumulatively they started to become a drag.

My favorite times of the year were the Smith School graduation ceremonies at the end of the fall and spring semesters. Twice a year, my senior staff and academic department directors would meet for a brief lunch at the basketball arena. We would then parade into the arena to the applause of our graduating students and their parents, relatives, and friends and parade onto a large stage. I would preside over the assembly. I would first welcome the crowd and then introduce undergraduate and MBA speakers. Next would come our commencement speaker, usually a prominent alum who would give a five to fifteen minute talk.

In my first semester as dean, I was the commencement speaker, and in my last semester, Bob Smith was the speaker. Ordinarily, Bob did not like to give graduation talks. "What can I say that is original?" he would ask. He did this one because it was my last. After the speaker would come the granting of the degrees. Students would march to the stage, where I would shake their hands and hand them a ceremonial scroll. We had nearly 1,000 graduates in the spring, so I would shake a lot of hands. At the end, I would give a short speech, close the ceremony, and the graduation stage party would march out.

I loved the ritual. The excitement of the group was tangible. My hand would be sore from shaking all those hands, but my spirits would be soaring. Better yet, the ceremonies would mark the end of the semester and the vacation time to follow.

Friends of the Library

I love books and have a major collection of science fiction and fantasy first editions. I mentioned this to the Dean of Libraries and gave him a personal tour through my collection when he visited my house for a Halloween party. A few months later, he asked my wife and me to join the board of directors of "Friends of the Library," a volunteer group organized to support the library.

We were delighted to do so. Other members of the board included several prominent book dealers, collectors, and library staff. Since the board met at members' homes as well as at the library, we offered to host a board meeting at our house, to the enjoyment of everyone attending.

When asked to become the chairman of the board, I accepted without delay. Being board chair was not a big deal. It meant running the board meetings, being a guest speaker at a few events, such as the annual library gala, and being present or speaking at some library functions. I was a reasonable but not great board chair. My primary allegiance was to the business school, and I couldn't devote much time to library fund raising.

One day, without notice, the entire organization disappeared. We were no longer notified of meetings (if there were any), there were no more friends-sponsored events, and no one told us about any changes. The organization was there one moment and gone the next. It was very strange, but as I was discovering, not uncharacteristic of university life—but I still wonder why no one told me of changes to come.

We Invade the World—
Part 1: Beijing

It started simply. We received a letter from the supposed representative of a distinguished Chinese university. The letter asked if we would like to explore a possible association with that institution.

It doesn't take a great intellect to know that business is global and that a leading business school should also have global connections. So, a few months later two of my associate deans departed for China to meet the representative and to visit the interested school.

When they returned, their trip report was disappointing. The targeted university knew nothing about us and the supposed agent was not their representative. But all was not bleak. They had met administrators from another well-known university. These people did want to start a relationship.

A plan and partnership emerged over the next year. We, Smith, would teach an Executive MBA program in Beijing. We would send a faculty member to China every month to teach a single course. Under this schedule, a student could complete the EMBA in eighteen months.

We would share revenues on a 50/50 basis. The Chinese school would be responsible for marketing and administration. We would be responsible for the curriculum and for teaching. The University of Maryland EMBA degree would be issued to students completing the program. Maryland admission criteria would be used to admit students.

Our president signed a Memorandum of Understanding, and the Chinese submitted the proposal for approval by the Chinese Ministry of Education. The proposal was approved, and we began operations. Our problems also began.

We sent people to China. We also needed to hire support people in China and pay salaries. It turned out that the university was incapable of sending a money wire transfer to Beijing. Admission applications didn't get approved. The graduate school didn't recognize many Chinese undergraduate universities, so graduates of these universities didn't meet Maryland standards. All students needed to pass English language proficiency tests. Only approved Maryland testers could test Chinese students, and these tests had to be administered in person. (Video conferencing was not acceptable!) We had to fly the testers to China, slowing down the testing process, delaying admittance, and increasing our costs.

In spite of these problems, we enrolled a first class of about sixty students. Cultural problems with our Chinese partners emerged. Chinese professors occasionally served as adjuncts for our courses when the topics included Chinese economics and markets. We were accustomed to getting student feedback about teaching quality via a course rating system. When attempting to ask our students to rate their Chinese instructors, the Chinese dean was violently opposed. "Chinese students do not rate their instructors," he told me. When we proceeded with the ratings anyway, the dean fired the individual administering the rating system. He told me "if I find out that she is put on the Maryland payroll, things will go badly for you."

Other problems emerged. Students were being rejected by Maryland that the Chinese considered excellent. It was taking too long to accept qualified students. Competition in Beijing was taking students away. A student could apply to another respected EMBA program, such as one offered by the University of Southern California, and could be interviewed in a day and accepted on the spot. We could not compete.

The second group of students enrolled in our program. Although there were fewer than forty individuals, we decided to increase our activities in China. We would hire our own people, assume responsibility for marketing and promotion, open a physical office, and expand in China. Boy, were we dumb!

We Invade the World— Part 2: Shanghai

We would open our own offices in Beijing and also expand our program to Shanghai. This meant that we would need staff in both cities. Rather that go it alone in Shanghai, we decided to partner with a China-based operation, the Maryland Center for China, which also represented the State of Maryland in the State's efforts to build trade between China and Maryland. We would locate our Shanghai office on their premises. In effect, they would be our general contractor, marketing the school, meeting with potential students, and handling our cash flow. (We were not licensed to send money out of China.)

Meanwhile, relations with our Beijing partner deteriorated. Their payments to us slowed. They constantly reminded us that we could only do business in China with their participation since that was our authorization from the Ministry of Education. Student recruiting of the third track had less than twenty students. We delayed the track for two months and then kicked it off in parallel with our first track in Shanghai.

We weren't entirely insane in launching our Shanghai program. Our largest expense was in sending faculty to China. With two programs, a professor could go to Beijing, teach a course, and then fly to Shanghai and teach the same course. Our net travel costs per course would therefore be lower since we would share the cost of international business class airfare across two courses.

The Maryland Center quickly discovered the inability of the university's graduate school to admit students. This problem, never corrected in spite of all of our efforts, would prove the ultimate demise of our international efforts.

We Invade the World— Part 3: Tunisia and Zurich

Smith was becoming recognized as an up and coming business school. We were promoting our international efforts and soon began receiving letters from many non-US schools proposing partnerships. Two that we pursued were a new school in Tunisia and an established operation in Zurich.

The Tunisia proposition was straightforward. We would offer an MS in Information Systems. They would market and recruit students using Maryland graduate student requirements. We would teach the classes and award the Maryland degree.

The partnership failed. We couldn't get enough students admitted for it to be financially viable. Along with the slowness of the graduate school in admitting students, a new problem emerged. Maryland does not recognize a three-year undergraduate degree. Unfortunately, many European schools are on a three-year schedule. Such students were automatically rejected.

We ran one track of the Tunisia MS. I then cancelled the program in spite of the rather lofty projections of some of my staff. I never did understand why Tunisia was strategic to the school, and since it wasn't, I was unwilling to continue to invest money in what might eventually become a marginal operation.

Zurich was very different. Its business school, a private commercial business, had been operating for some time. It had a variety of partners but had recently ended a partnership with a US school and was looking for a new one. They made the following proposal. Courses would be offered in both Zurich and the US. Zurich would recruit students, we would offer a dual degree (Maryland and Zurich) for completion of a combined program. Our faculty would teach courses in Zurich and at Maryland. This seemed like an excellent idea. We would be paid on a per student basis and our expenses would be reimbursed. The partnership would give us a base in an excellent location and would extend our reach. We also envisioned that students from Zurich and the US could take courses in China, thus creating a global footprint for Smith.

It turned out that the University of Maryland did not believe in dual degrees, even though I showed them examples of dual degrees being offered by the world's best universities. We revised the approach to offer two degrees based on completing the requirements of a Zurich degree and a Smith degree. We executed a Memorandum of Understanding and launched the program.

All sorts of problems emerged. Swiss students were taking classes before they had been admitted to the program by the Maryland graduate school. Students were being told by Zurich that they were admitted to the program even though our graduate school had not processed their applications. The graduate school was rejecting students because graduate school personnel didn't understand the Swiss educational system. The Zurich people didn't understand the Smith education requirements and refused to respond to our demands that they adjust the program to meet our requirements. The same delays experienced in China and Tunisia were again taking place. This time, however, the problems were even more serious because there were numerous applications and not enough graduate school staff to process them.

A bitter battle over the contents of a course being taught in Zurich in German but used as part of the Smith degree emerged. We were adamant that the course must be taught in English and also meet out academic specifications. They ignored us. After the Swiss dean suggested that we cover up the fact that the course was being taught in German, I concluded that the partnership was impossible. I sent the Zurich school a letter terminating our agreement in accordance with its terms. Zurich stopped paying our bills and sent us a letter claiming that they had been damaged by us. We negotiated for months with no overall resolution. In the end, we followed the terms of the original agreement until the agreement expired. When the end date was reached, the program was discontinued.

About the same time, having graduated all of the students enrolled in our China programs, we ceased program activities there. We had invaded the world, experienced the euphoria of early success, become frustrated by our inability to serve an international base, and had finally decided to retreat to our own home shores.

Strategic Planning Retreats

Each November, the top 30–35 faculty and staff would retreat for a strategy session to discuss topics vital to the success of the strategic plan. We would form study groups in September to address key topics, discuss their findings at the retreat, and assign follow-on activities requiring more study.

I managed this process, created the agenda, and picked the study teams. Each retreat began with a set of "Axioms" (directions that were to be accepted as gospel without debate).

Axioms for the Retreat

Growth

Pursue the goals of regional dominance, and national and international prominence through growth. Growth in:

- Programs (size, number, scope, and reputation)
- Faculty (number and depth in each academic discipline—increase the "bench")
- Facility (annex, technology, and physical improvements to original wing AND off-campus sites)
- External relationships (number and quality by region and industry for alumni, corporate partners, other departments on campus)

Change

Understand the competition in the marketplace and the changes necessitated by its dynamics. We must responsibly but aggressively challenge convention in our programs, curriculum, and views of business education to maintain a proactive approach to change.

- Importance of effecting change through pilot projects and experimentation
- Continually assess the extent to which our products and processes meet our needs, goals, and market expectations

Thought Leadership/Research Excellence

Pursue excellence in the generation and dissemination of knowledge, in keeping with the campus goal of becoming a top research institution. We must leverage the central tenet of research prominence in both traditional and novel ways to enhance all facets of our programs and outreach.

- Importance of aiming at the best and most competitive research outlets and forums
- Increased emphasis on potential impact of the research themes
- The need for integrating the expertise of and research accomplishments of our faculty with marketing the Smith brand
- Importance of leveraging cutting-edge research for enhancing our curriculum
- The use of Centers as enablers of the research mission and contributors to an intellectual climate that is unique to the Smith School

Integration of Technology

Integrate technology in innovative and boundary-expanding ways to deliver on the expectations created by the branding campaign. We must assume a visible leadership role in using technology to push conventional boundaries and to prepare students for the challenges of technology change and adoption.

- Use of technology broadly across the curriculum
- Gain respect for reliable and consistent delivery
- Create a playpen for prototypes and experimentation
- Continue to enrich the technology–curriculum link
- Expand partnership with technology firms as both clients and suppliers

Innovation and Entrepreneurship

Create, foster, and sustain a climate for innovation and entrepreneurship.

- Importance of a structure and established expectation to innovate in curriculum, programs, outreach, technological tools, and applications
- Continue to generate new product or process concepts

Linkages and Teamwork

Constantly explore and seek mutually enhancing relationships among various units or operations of the Smith School in such a way as to enhance the overall intellectual capital and asset base of the Smith School

- Create internal and external processes for sharing and communication
- Build new partnerships in pursuit of entrepreneurial goals

Each retreat would open more questions than were resolved. Here are some questions from one early retreat.

- Should we begin to gather school wide metrics such as citations, editorial boards, editors and associate editors, etc.?
- Should our promotion program give more emphasis towards corporations and executives? If so, what should we reduce?
- Is there enough faculty research funding for major research projects? Should these projects be funded by external contracts and grants or should the school fund some of these? If the school, how much and what process should be used for awards to faculty?
- Is there sufficient emphasis in the annual faculty merit review on impact rather than number counting for publications? How can high-impact books and articles aimed at disseminating research to a broad business/practitioner audience be better recognized?
- What requirements for PhD students can be reduced to give students more time for research and publishing?
- Can we distinguish halo/brand from quality in competitors?
- What research culture/product are we turning out?
- Should we have a specific target (e.g., 10%) for PhD student placement in top institutions?
- Should we create a composite b-school ranking (from the major publications) for specific Smith school quality targets?

- What is the ideal student candidate profile? How can we integrate this ideal profile into the selection process?
- Should we create specific teams of undergraduate students (e.g., an IT Corps) to help departments and faculty transition towards e-Smith?
- How shall we integrate our research center and executive education plans to take our intellectual property to market?
- What part of our courses should be on the web (more than just syllabi)? Should there be a plan of what we are going to do, by when, and why?
- What should be the plan for faculty mentorship of our undergraduate Freshman Scholars Program?
- How do we package our cross-functional research accomplishments to leverage our promotion and reputation-building activities?
- What cross-functional themes should we promote at the school (rather than department) level?
- What mechanisms are there to pool resources to support cross-functional research?
- How do we coordinate our cross-functional concentrations? Should there be lead departments, centers, or faculty?
- What academic purpose do the concentrations serve?
- How do we reduce and rationalize our concentrations and elective offerings?
- What electives and concentrations should we support at our various locations?
- What is the impact of our cross-functional concentrations on placement?
- What is the relationship between our centers and the curriculum offerings and how do we package these for maximum advantage?
- How do we define the Smith brand?
- What is the marketing strategy to build the Smith brand?
- What are the top 50 corporate prospects for sources of capital?

- How shall we integrate our research center and executive education plans to take our intellectual property to market?
- How do we package our cross-functional research accomplishments to leverage our promotion and reputation-building activities?

Study teams would address many of these questions during the school year, and others would be the subjects of future retreats.

I decided we should devoted one retreat to benchmark the Smith School against our competitors. We would study the best five to seven business schools whose quality we believed we could meet or exceed. To choose the benchmark schools, I asked each of our department chairs to identify our ten top competitors. Our senior administrators took the same challenge. I then chose seven schools that were on both top ten lists.

Every program would analyze each of the competitor's programs. Our undergraduate office would analyze their undergraduate offices; our graduate program offices would analyze theirs; and each academic department would examine the other's academic departments. We would also examine their finance and administrative efforts, their promotion activities, their career centers, and their IT operations. The study groups would report their findings at the retreat and recommend improvements to our programs gleaned from our competitors.

The schools we benchmarked included USC, Carnegie Mellon, North Carolina at Chapel Hill, NYU, and the University of California at Berkeley.

Chapter 7

For the Good of Us

The Smith Fellows Program

Many insights emerged from the retreat. One, in particular, produced a transformational concept for our undergraduate program. We concluded that the University of North Carolina at Chapel Hill (UNC) and NYU had superior undergraduate programs. North Carolina had far fewer students (a total of about 550) and NYU funded its undergraduate activities at levels far beyond Smith's. Both schools, therefore, could provide many more resources to their undergraduate student than we could.

Rather than accept the current reality as a long-term limitation, I decided to create an entirely new concept for our program. We couldn't reduce our student body to North Carolina's size. We were nearly four times larger. However, our scale had a strategic advantage: UNC had smart students. We had smart students but many more!

We could probably never equal NYU's financial capabilities, but we were proving that we could raise a lot of money. In the next few years, we could target our funds raising efforts to the undergraduate program.

Money could give us the ability to build a large number of improvements and options for our students. We would create a "Smith Fellows Program," where every student at Smith could get a special experience. Each student would be invited to join one or two tracks of thirty to thirty-five students to study a special area. There would be as many as thirty tracks. For example, thirty students would be paid $5,000 per year to work as research assistants for faculty members. Another group would be given specialized training in the use of financial software. A third, smaller group, would manage an investment fund under the guidance of a faculty member.

In essence, we would be building a number of small colleges with the Smith School. Our size would allow students to have many options throughout their academic careers, and we could offer a far superior set of options to those of any small school.

I committed the school to the new program. Being an optimist, I requested assistance from the university. After all, this was a major educational advance, in line with the university's strategic goals. We crafted a plan and sent it as a proposal to the university. Here is what we proposed.

The Smith Fellows Program

Competition for the best and brightest students among top-ranked business schools is extremely high. The Robert H. Smith School undergraduate program has achieved excellence but needs to expand its range of distinctive and quality programs in order to move from excellence to greatness. Special programs currently offered by the Smith School, such as Quest and Business Honors, reach only a small fraction of the highly talented freshman class entering each year. *The goal of the Smith Fellows Program is to provide a special program for **all of our directly admitted freshmen and sophomores** and then to offer these students, as well as **all UMCP internal and external transfer students,** special programs during the Junior and Senior years.* The Smith Undergraduate Program is currently ranked #20 by *U.S. News and World Reports.* Our objective for the program is to be among the top 10 undergraduate programs in the United States.

In his September 13, 2004 address to the University, "Taking Stock: State of the University," the President stated:

"I strongly believe that every student should have the opportunity for a special program experience. We're not quite there yet, but we'll be there soon ...

My personal view is that international experience should be a high priority for all our students. In 2004 one cannot be fully educated without an understanding of the values and circumstances of other cultures that can only be acquired through first hand experience. There is no replacing being there."

The Smith Fellows program will begin in the freshman year with the Smith Freshman/Sophomore Fellows Program during the Academic Year 2006/07. **All freshmen** directly admitted to the Smith undergraduate program (approximately 300 per year) will be included. These students will participate as a cohort in a broad range of academic and co-curricular activities that will enrich their education and create a strong bond of community among the members of the class. During AY 2005/06, courses will be redesigned and a variety of aspects of the new Fellows Program will be tested.

The Freshman Fellows will be introduced early in their academic careers to the distinctive features of Smith School's approach to business education and research. Students will gain an appreciation of cutting-edge research and development in the rapidly converging business and technology fields. This will link directly to the vision of the university as the leading research university in the region. Going beyond the traditional research apprenticeship model of faculty–student interactions, shared experiences will be designed to bring faculty and students together, so that students can be exposed to the principles and values of scholarly research, and the role of faculty in translating their research findings into business practice. In this way, the notion of research is demonstrated within the business environment and students will appreciate why business practice is both the source and beneficiary of research conducted by the top business schools. The experiential components of this key theme will range from single events to year-long projects (examples listed below include film series and field trips that highlight faculty–student shared experiences.) Further, a significant number of students will be given the opportunity to gain international experience in keeping with the President's objectives.

As part of the Freshman/Sophomore Fellows Program, the Smith School will redesign its current academic program, expand undergraduate advising, and develop a group of co-curricular activities such as summer orientation, film series, field trips, monthly socials, an emerging leaders retreat, service projects, special career training and events and international study trips. The introductory BMGT 110 course will be revamped completely and will include two new core topics: Business ethics and the impact of technology on business practices. In this way, the Smith School will place additional emphasis on two themes in which it continues to pursue a leadership role.

During the sophomore year, the Smith Fellows will be introduced to the **Junior/Senior Fellows Program** with the goal that all students will have the opportunity to participate in one or more special opportunities for which they are qualified. The goal of the Junior/Senior Year Fellows Program is to offer all students at least one special experience. To achieve this goal, existing programs will be expanded or modified and new programs and initiatives will be launched. These include:

- Doubling the size of the Smith School Honors Program.
- Moving from its current experimental stage to full-scale implementation of the Smith Technology Scholars Program.
- Initiating a Smith Faculty Research Fellows Initiative.
- Completing the revision of the General Business Major and implementing an Entrepreneurship Track within it.
- Introducing a Smith Six Sigma Fellows Program.
- Moving from ad hoc international field trips to a full scale International Fellows Program, possibly in conjunction with the current revision of the International Business Major.
- Continuing and expanding the Smith Talent Acquisition and Referral System (STARS) for mentoring and recruiting minority high school students.

- Creating focused special experiences in each of our academic departments, laboratories and research centers.
- Creating a unique Junior/Senior Transfer Student Honors Program with honors level courses and scholarship support.

Requirements and Financial Support Needed

The creation and full-scale implementation of the Smith Fellow Program will require substantial resources. We propose to fund the majority of the costs of the program from the Smith School's operating budgets and development activities. We are requesting university support in two areas: 1) the hiring of two faculty in AY 2006 and an additional two faculty in AY 2007 and 2) the hiring of one undergraduate advisor in each of AY 2006 and AY 2007. This would require base budget increases of approximately $300,000 in each of AY 2006 and AY 2007.

Freshman/Sophomore Fellows Program
1. Tenure Track Faculty (2) for Freshman/Sophomore Program: $250,000
2. Academic Advisor (1): $50,000
3. Faculty Director Overload: $25,000
4. Travel funds for student trips: $50,000 per year.
5. Additional Scholarship Support for DirectAdmits:AY '07:$100,000; AY '08: $200,000; AY '09: $300,000; Long Term: $1,000,000 per year.

Junior/Senior Fellows Program
1. Tenure Track Faculty for Expanded Honors and Entrepreneurship Programs (2): $250,000
2. Funding for Smith Technology Scholars Initiative: $125,000 per year for student support; $250,000 per year for staff; $125,000 per year for technology and data support.
3. Funding for 50 students for Smith Research Initiative@ $5,000/ student: $250,000 per year
4. Additional Academic Advisor: $50,000

5. Travel funds for the Smith International Scholars Program: $50,000 per year.
6. Staff member for STARS program: $50,000
7. Scholarship Funds for the Transfer Student Honors Program: $100,000 per year.

Smith Fellows Program Financial Requirements

Area	2006	2007	2008	2009	Goal
School	125,000	750,000	750,000	750,000	750,000
University (Base Budget)	2 Faculty + 1 Advisor $300,000	2 Faculty + 1 Advisor $300,000			
Annual Contributions	350,000	250,000	250,000	250,000	100,000
Scholarship Endowment + Operating Funds					20,000,000

Appendix: Details of the Freshman/Sophomore Fellows Program

1. Eligibility: All students directly admitted to the Robert H. Smith of Business as freshmen will be designated as Smith Fellows.
2. Academic Program: All courses "F"-version, restricted to BMGT – 14 cr.
   a. BMGT 110F (or BMGT 101F) – Keystone – 3 credits – 1st semester
      i. Course review and revision to include information systems, logistics and supply chain management and incorporating experiential learning opportunities and field trips. An innovative approach to business ethics

and the role of business within society will also be incorporated.

    ii. Ideally, 4 sections @ 60 students/section plus one CPS/BSE section @ 80 (serving 40–60 BMGT majors) to cover the cohort.

    iii. Fridays – schedule 2-hour "discussion" sections staffed by graduate assistants.

b. UNIV 100F (or BMGT 100F) – Home room – 1 credit – 1st semester

    i. Staffed by undergraduate advisors, with registration corresponding to advising assignments plus concurrent with BMGT 110 section.

    ii. Four 2-hour sessions/semester to address UNIV 100 issues plus registration/advising with remaining time dedicated to review sessions and to co-curricular activities.

    iii. Scheduled time facilitates joint activities, field trips etc.

    iv. Enrollment would be for all business students (optional for BMGT majors in College Park Scholars or University Honors because students in CPS and University Honors enroll in another UNIV 100.)

c. BMGT 367F – 1 credit – Ideally 5 sections of 60

    i. Offered to Smith Fellows in 2nd semester of the sophomore year, with special career programming such as etiquette program, communications and job skills training.

3. Special co-curricular programming:

a. Develop two-day summer orientation program, with special programming on second day, and kick-off full program day ending with the Freshman Convocation in 1st week of the semester

b. Develop special co-curricular program opportunities, such as:

      i. Film Series – associated with UNIV 110/BMGT 110. Hold receptions following with faculty commentators. The Smith School Gateway Club (a group of 30–50 undergraduate students) would be involved in these activities.

     ii. Field Trips:

        1. DC Culture Vultures – Smithsonian: Sackler-Freer & National Art Galleries; get a docent, 1st semester

        2. Service project – end of spring 2nd semester

        3. New York field trip – perhaps multiple destinations: stock exchange, museums/art galleries, advertising agencies—given programming opportunities – 3rd semester

        4. Special career event – Etiquette dinner plus – networking reception – 4th semester

        5. Monthly socials – Hosted by Gateway Club

    iii. Freshman Emerging Leaders Retreat – 2nd semester (good basis for service event end of term)

    iv. Speaker Series

    v. International Study Trip(s) for course credit

***

We didn't expect to get much support from the university. I'm not even sure anyone at the university level read the proposal. So when no money came, we launched the program using our own funds. The launch took two years. By the third year, the program was in full operation with close to twenty-five tracks in the Junior and Senior years.

The Smith Fellows Program appears to be a revolutionary new concept in undergraduate business education. Our students love it. And our faculty loves the program too. This program will take the undergraduate program to greatness.

I, personally, was committed to the program. I had been planning to complete my second 5-year appointment as dean and then step down from the deanship to join the faculty. Ten years as dean was more than enough. But as the Fellows Program emerged, I decided that it needed a committed dean to guide it through its initial years. Therefore, I told the provost that I would like to extend my appointment for another 5-year term (even though I intended to serve only two additional years.) This meant that I would have another 5-year review.

Chapter 8

Us Versus Them

Breaking the Campus Catering Monopoly

Many universities have outsourced their food services operations to commercial suppliers. Maryland has not. It operates a campus catering business. The food is poor but expensive. Their staff is slow and inefficient.

Because my usual lunch fare was a tuna fish sandwich eaten at my desk, I was unaware of the poor but expensive food until I heard deans complaining at our monthly deans meeting. I became more aware after we contracted with them to install and operate a lunchroom in the South Wing Addition to Van Munching Hall. The addition was completed on schedule, but eight months later, the lunchroom had not yet opened. I decided that I needed to rid us of the campus operation.

I asked my associate dean to send the following memo:

To Director of Dining Services
According to the Memorandum of Understanding entered into between the Department of Dining Services and the Robert H. Smith School of Business last spring, the Facility was to be opened on "... approximately July 1, 2002." The Facility includes that area referred to as "Rudy's Café" in room 1517.

Eight months have expired since the promised time for opening the facility. We have made numerous verbal and written requests of you and ACE as to the time when the facility will be opened. We still have no idea when the facility will open. The delay is having a negative impact on the School. I remind you that we are paying for much of the financing of this space, which is not yet operational.

This is to notify you that unless the Facility, and in particular Rudy's Café, is fully operational by March 31, 2003, we will consider Dining Services to be in material breach of our agreement and will proceed to take advantage of other options for use of the space as a dining facility.

The Café, along with an "Executive Dining Room" opened a few months later. Students and faculty used the Café while the Executive Dining Room was used to provide catered lunches and dinners for our EMBA program and for special events. The situation might have remained that way for years had not Dining Services been so poor. We would ask them to put bottled water and soda in six rooms. They would send us a bill for $1,000. Our MBA students, who were having an evening social on the business school's lawn, were chased away by the police after Dining Services called police to report that the students were serving beer.

I directed my associate dean to write another memo. It included the following paragraphs:

1. You called the police on our MBAs which I find to be personally offensive, sneaky and cowardly. There is no difference between their using bottles and cans in the restricted and monitored area from what goes on at Saturday tailgates which I made clear. If the harassment continues, I will make that point all over campus, to friends I have in the State's Attorney's office, to neighbors and friends of mine who serve on the Board of Regents and to friends I have in the Legislature.

2. Our staff tells us that your prices tend to be outrageous and confiscatory. An example is a charge of $1,000 for water and sodas at a relatively small and short reception. I believe that person went elsewhere.

3. We have no intention of using dining services other than as required under our current contract with you.

It is unfortunate that I have to be this blunt but that is the way it is. Have a good weekend.

There was no progress, so I issued a directive to the school:

You are not to use Dining Services for any School events (other than those in Rudy's or the Executive Dining Room) without the express written permission of the Dean's Office.

I then directed that we write another memo to Dining Services exercising our rights to buy out their ownership of Rudy's Café and the Executive Dining Room for the value of their capital investments in the facility, as specified in their contract with the Smith School. In the commercial world, such a transaction would have concluded our association. In academia, nothing is so simple. Weeks later, we received a response that they had taken the issue to the provost and the university's finance committee. We would be allowed to buy out the facility, but in addition to the capital investments, each year we would have to pay the university their lost profits on the operation.

I then demanded what I really wanted—the food service rights to the Executive Dining Room and the rest of the building. They could keep Rudy's (I really didn't want to run a cafeteria), but I wanted the right to use external caterers in other areas of the school. They accepted this "compromise." It cost us nothing except that another campus group now hated us. We had liberated the school!

Launching the EMBA

The school had at one time investigated the possibility of launching an Executive MBA (EMBA) program. It had decided that the market was too small to make this worthwhile. Early in my deanship, our

Executive Programs Center would again raise the topic. At that time, the center was not well managed and I was reluctant to allow the center to offer any degree-granting program, since these require both rigor and control.

Several years passed. I replaced the management of the center (twice) and believed that I had hired the right people to run executive education. The EMBA was back on the table, and I agreed to the program.

Launching a new degree program requires a number of steps. Various university committees must approve the degree proposal. The Board of Regents must approve both the degree and the proposed tuition. These steps could take a year or more. The program would then have to be marketed, students enrolled, and finally, courses could be taught. This could add as much as another year.

My operating style, once a decision had been made, was "do it now." We decided to begin marketing the program before the program had been approved. I instructed the staff to include a few caveats in our marketing materials such as a footnote indicating that the "tuition was tentative." In their enthusiasm to get the program going, my caveats were either forgotten or ignored. We began television advertising and solicited applications through a website. Once again, the provost chastised us (this time deservedly).

As I learned to my dismay in August, you are now advertising on your web site and in other media your proposed new Executive MBA program, which has not yet been formally considered or approved by the campus. When we spoke about this at our meeting on August 8, I told you specifically that the program could only be advertised as "pending approval", and that all those expressing interest in the program should be informed of its non-approved status. Your web site and your other forms of advertising, however, continue to omit this qualification.

What's worse, your web site advertises a program which will consider applications from individuals who do not have an undergraduate degree, in direct conflict with campus policy applying to all graduate programs.

In addition, your web site and other advertising states a tuition of $67,500 for the program, a figure that has not been approved either by the campus or the Board of Regents, who must approve all such charges for University programs. There is not even any agreement between the Smith School and the campus on revenue sharing should such a tuition rate be approved by the campus and the Board of Regents.

I directed my staff to make the appropriate changes and responded to the provost:

All offending information has been eliminated. In particular, the program and start date are marked pending approval, the tuition and application fee sections are no longer there. There is no reference to admission without an undergraduate degree and what had been previously called an application is now listed as "statement of qualification." This should solve all of the earlier issues and still allow us the flexibility to move forward without committing anyone.

The program was approved and the Regents confirmed the proposed tuition. I negotiated a revenue sharing agreement with the campus. They would take 5% of our revenues. We would keep 95%. Admissions for our first EMBA track went well, and we admitted about thirty students for the program. The program, designed to be taught Friday–Sundays over eighteen months, would generate over $1 million in revenues the first year and close to $2 million in the second year. It would also become the model for our future offerings in Switzerland and China. Today, the EMBA is a respected, mature program having been ranked in the top twenty-five by the *Financial Times*, the *Wall Street Journal,* and *Business Week*.

Overloads Everywhere

Teaching with tenured or tenure track professors is expensive. Half of a professor's effort is expected to be research. Therefore, professors have low teaching requirements at elite business schools. The typical, research active professor at the Smith School teaches three courses per year. New hires are often given a one-course reduction during their first year as Smith. An assistant professor's primary focus is creating a research portfolio worthy of tenure. Also, recent graduates are inexperienced teachers, making it difficult for them to teach in the MBA program. MBA students are very demanding and rip inexperienced teachers apart.

Our expanding part-time MBA programs placed great demands on our teaching capacity, especially on the associate and full professors. Each new track would add seventeen courses to our teaching requirements. In steady state we were teaching seven part-time and three full-time tracks as well as one to two Executive MBA tracks and courses in China and Switzerland. We were hiring about ten new professors per year. This added to our capacity, but we had to meet our needs through "overloads."

An overload is an extra course taught after a professor has taught his or her normal teaching load. The faculty member is paid 10% of his nine-month salary for this service. It's a nice way for a faculty member to earn extra money, and it's great for the school because a 10% payment is a relatively inexpensive way to acquire course coverage.

Authorizing overloads required an extended series of transactions. An overload document was created. It had to be signed by the faculty member, reviewed by my assistant dean for administration, approved by me, and then sent to the provost's office for his approval. Because all of these steps had to be completed before the extra course was actually taught, I was constantly asking the provost to approve late overload requests.

One day, I arrived for my monthly meeting with the provost. I had no significant issues to discuss and didn't know of any that he had with the business school. I was shocked when he jumped all over me. I am paraphrasing the following: "Do you know what you've done? You've paid $2 million dollars to faculty without university approval. You've violated university policy and created a scandal. If anybody finds out, the president could be fired!"

The provost then dropped in front of me a list of professors, dates, and overload payments. The provost added: "No wonder your faculty loves you. You've bought them. I want to see every overload approval for every extra dollar you've paid. And, if you make any up, I will fire you!"

I was shaken. I knew that the provost had approved every overload payment. So why was there an issue? While $2 million is a large number, our total faculty payroll was over $25 million, so $2 million was a relatively small percentage of the total.

What had gone wrong? Why was this being brought up now when we had been paying overloads for years? My guess was that like many other issues at Maryland, things had been ignored until someone had noticed the magnitude of the activity. Then, they panicked.

I returned to my office, called my assistant dean, swore her to secrecy, and worked out a timetable to put the required documents together. Over the next week, she assembled a carton of overloads. I reviewed every one. Every overload had been properly executed and signed by the provost. The school had done nothing wrong.

After we sent the package to the provost, I met with him again. He said that we needed to put limits on faculty payments. We agreed to limits as a percentage of a professor's nine-month salary. He didn't raise any issues about our package, and the scandal talk was not repeated. I stated that I had a complaint. I said that I had been insulted by his insinuation that I might make up overload documents. He apologized!

I walked out of his office angrier than when I walked in. What a crummy way to deal with people.

Relations with Other Parts of Campus

We were disliked or hated on Campus outside of the business school. Much was driven by jealousy. Much was driven by the mistaken notion that we were consuming an unfair percentage of campus resources. Part was because we had the best students, with the highest graduation rates. We also had the best facilities. You couldn't find a favorable opinion anywhere. Every battle I had fought created a new detractor, but the way I saw it, if I didn't fight, they would walk all over us.

Everything we did was treated with suspicion. I had heard many negative comments about the school in general and me in particular. It came to a head in a report prepared by a committee commissioned to review my second five-year term as dean. They wrote: "... the Smith School has become incredibly isolated from the rest of the campus in terms of following policies and procedures. They frequently want to do things in ways other than the accepted campus procedure, claiming that they require an exception because of their unusual situation.

"The pattern is that the Smith School does something without asking campus advice as to the best way to do it. Consequently, a great deal of time and effort must be spent to fix the problem the Smith School has caused. This is typical of their 'go it alone approach' in administrative matters in general. ... We were told by several persons that 'when something comes over from the Smith School, we give it especially close scrutiny.'"

The many negative comments in the report led me to write a rebuttal:

> To the provost:
> I am in receipt of the Report of the Committee to review my performance dated April 27, 2006. I appreciate the efforts that the Committee expended to create this report and am in agreement with many of its conclusions and recommendations. I would, however, like to correct some misstatements and misunderstandings made either by the Committee or the individuals that they interviewed.

The Committee stated

"During the years of financial exigency, the dean abruptly severed cooperative ties with several of the colleges. The program with Arts and Humanities and the relationship between the Dingman Center and the Clark School are two examples that surfaced during this review."

In reality, in the 2003 academic year, the school executed a three-year agreement with ARHU regarding the Business, Language and Cultures Program (BCL). The agreement called for a one-year notification period in the event that either party wished to terminate the program. In early 2004, we notified ARHU that we would be terminating the program approximately 18 months from that date. This notification was hardly abrupt and our reason for termination was not financial but rather the poor quality of the program and lack of preparation of ARHU students for business courses because they were not taking the prerequisite core business classes. At the meeting in which we informed ARHU of our intent to terminate, we suggested alternatives and have jointly designed two replacement programs that will be launched in the coming academic year.

The Committee's reference to the Dingman Center also misstates actual circumstances. During 2002–2004 working relations between the Center and the Clark School deteriorated because of several personnel factors. Because of my own dissatisfaction with the Center's performance, in Spring 2004, I replaced the management of the Center and restructured its operations. This restructuring has been a tremendous success and today, there are both engineering and business students active in Dingman Center activities.

I know of no other cooperative programs or cooperative efforts that we have severed or modified although an attempted program with Life Sciences under a former dean failed to materialize because of lack of interested students. Indeed, programs like Quest, the MS in Telecommunications, and our joint appointments with ISR and UMIACS are thriving.

The Committee, in Appendix 9, reports statements by several deans such as

"He has captured an unreasonable fraction of resources of the university for his college."... "He takes what he can and never gives back."

I find a statement like this completely inaccurate and unfair. First, the business school has not received any material increase in funding from the campus since I have been dean. Funding was added to field the Shady Grove undergraduate program but this funding disappeared during the budget cut period. Indeed, our revenue growth has been self-generated and during the three years of budget cuts, the business school's budget cuts were on its total revenues, and were more than two times the average cut to other academic units. This helped other units retain more of their base budget, a fact not known or accepted by other units. Also, the business school received a total of $50,000 (of about $10 million) of one-time funds from the Provost and APAC to help various schools absorb the budget cuts leaving more support for the other colleges.

I have also attempted to be a good Campus citizen both as a dean and as an individual. I served on the board and as president of Friends of the Libraries for several years. Additionally, my relationship with Robert H. Smith has helped the university generate substantial gifts for the Performing Arts Center as well as other non-business school activities. I could detail a list of activities I have been involved with for the Campus but I don't think that such a list would be useful.

I must add that I am deeply disappointed by the stated opinions of my colleagues and am especially taken aback by statements about "lack of trust" and "integrity" since I do not believe there is any basis in fact for these comments. I do recognize that their beliefs are real to them and that a conscious effort is needed to realign them for the good of the Campus.

    Sincerely,

    Howard Frank

    Dean

Despite the negative comments from elsewhere on campus, reviews from the Smith School were very positive and my record of accomplishments was extraordinary. The committee voted "unanimously and enthusiastically" to reappoint me another five- year term.

I met with the provost to discuss the report. He informed me that he and the president agreed: **They would not offer me another 5-year term.** It was clear that they were fed up, not with my performance, but with my style. They no longer wanted someone who would rock the boat.

On my part, I was fed up with the university—its bureaucratic processes and procedures; its president who said the right things, but when you asked for help, gave you only air; its provost, whose erratic interference caused frequent conflicts because I wouldn't accept his micromanagement; jealous backbiting deans and inept staff who slowed us down whenever we tried to do something new.

I would be happy to leave, I thought, but since I still had nearly a year remaining on my current appointment, I said I didn't want to be a lame duck. The provost offered to extend my appointment by one year and announce to the university at large that my appointment was being extended. In the announcement he wouldn't mention the term length. I accepted his offer.

This was an obvious gimmick to get rid of me without seeming to have fired me. I didn't realize at that time that I would need to keep secret the terms of my new appointment. I would have to pretend that I would be in the job up to five to six more years even though I would be leaving in less than two.

Early Termination

The school had negotiated the following agreement for MBA tuition with the university. The university would keep the bulk of full-time MBA tuition payments. The business school would keep 75% of payments that exceeded a specified number of students. We would keep the fees paid by full-time students. The business school would retain tuition and fee payments from its off campus part-time MBA programs.

Tuition rates were approved annually by the Board of Regents and were submitted about a year in advance. Fees were considered to be a local matter. The goal of fees was to cover the cost of doing business, so every year we would submit a proposal for the next year's fees to the provost. The proposal would include a cost justification for the fees. Our fees were lower than our costs and didn't cover the full cost of offering the MBA programs.

Because the cost to the student was the sum of tuition and fees, it was irrelevant to them whether we increased fees or tuition. On the other hand, we would keep all of the fees but virtually none of the tuition for full-time MBA students. Year after year, I had been following a strategy of increasing fees but not increasing tuition. Year after year my proposals for tuition and fees were routinely approved. This changed when I received the following e-mail.

Howard:

I will not approve your request for MBA/MS student fee increases. This is because a) the requested increases are enormous (generally around 18–60%) and b) these are really tuition increases, but you are requesting them because, unlike a tuition increase, you don't have to share the revenue with the campus.

My response:

Are you referring to both the full and part time increases? As you know, the part time program is completely self-supporting; we don't share the tuition with the campus and are making major facilities investments in DC ($1.5 million in facilities alone) as well as have additional expenses in both Shady Grove and Baltimore. We are also extending career services to part time students and investing in additional technology.

As for the full-time program, we are bringing on line a $19.5 million facility of which 25% will be dedicated to the MBA students. The campus is not paying anything towards this investment and the business school is responsible for $13.5 million in cash.

I failed to add that the overall cost of the part-time program is not going up by 18–60% but only one component of the cost is going up by this amount. The actual total cost of the program would be going up by 7.8% in Shady Grove, 6.0% in Baltimore, and 6.5% in D.C.

Another e-mail was waiting for me the next day:

You have played this game for many years, with the result that for a full-time MBA student at College Park total fees now exceed tuition by a good margin. For example, for an In-State, full-time, College Park MBA student taking 15 credit hours in a semester, tuition for that semester is now $7227 and total fees are $8630. The tuition alone is approximately twice the College Park graduate tuition figure for in-state students, and that is the only charge that is shared with the campus. The remaining fees you propose are as follows:

Student Charge (an interesting name!) – $358 per credit hour – up 25%
College Park site fee (a site fee at College Park?) – $169 per credit hour – up 25%
MBAA Club Activities Fee – $225 – up 28.5%

Other fees you have requested are:

Shady Grove site fee – $130 per credit hour – up 60%
Baltimore site fee – $100 per credit hour – up 41%

For 2007–08, you propose to raise $11,270,254 by fees alone. Did you request a tuition increase for 2007–08?

I tried to maintain my cool with this reply:

This conversation should have been held before this e-mail exchange but here's the answers to your questions and concerns.

Since we get no operational $ from campus for the MBA programs or service improvements, we have been funding these through the fees. You question an MBA site fee in College Park. Not counting the cash the school paid for the South Wing addition in 2002, we've been paying $1,900,000 per year in debt service per year in College Park. We also paid $2,848,000 for technology, $1,933,000 for our Career Center, $2,339,000 for our MBA office and $944,000 in MBA scholarships (of which $500,000 comes from the campus.)

We are also investing $1,500,000 in DC for facilities and about $400,000 for Shady Grove/Baltimore facilities. In addition, we spend close to $2,000,000/year to market the school and the programs, which result in the revenues being generated by the part time program.

We calculate that it costs us about $36,000/year to educate a full-time MBA student. That is, if we retained all of our full-time tuitions, we would break even on full-time out of state MBA students and lose money on every in-state full-time student. We do not retain all of our MBA tuition and we do not receive any state support for in-state students and of course, the university retains the standard graduate rates for the full-time program.

In-state MBA students receive substantial services beyond the typical campus graduate student at no cost to the university. These include career services, student team rooms and lounges, and access to state of the art technology in the labs. The funds for this have to come from somewhere. To date they have been coming from the MBA fees which as of yet are not yet equal to the cost of providing these services. By the way, the MBA Club Fee is not retained by the Smith School but rather is given to the MBA Student Association which is an elected body that provides cultural and social services to MBA students (e.g., running an Asia week and supporting the nearly 20 MBA clubs like the Black MBA Association, etc.)

You are nearly correct in our expectation for fee revenue in 2008. Our actual projection is $10,327,149. The $11,270,255 that you refer to is our **forecast of costs** is $11,270,255.

We have not requested a tuition increase for the coming year.

You point out that we have followed the same strategy regarding fees for many years. You are correct and therefore your turning down the fee increase comes as even more of a surprise **since you have NEVER mentioned or discussed with me that you had any problems or issues with this strategy**. In fact, each year we have pointed out that the fee increase strategy was being followed to bring our costs in line with the revenues of the program. No one has ever expressed problems with this strategy.

Moreover, the total proposed College Park full time MBA fee increase comes to $106 per credit hour or $2862 per student per year. If this full amount had been implemented as a tuition rather than a fee increase, according to our differential tuition plan, the campus would keep 25% or $715 per student per year. **The total $ lost to campus, based on our expected number of full time students would therefore be, at most, $171,005.** Therefore, I sincerely request that you revisit your decision based on this additional information.

From the provost:

> Actually, you have not requested a tuition increase since 2005. The reason I have decided to reject your proposal this year is that your requested increases were so large that I decided to go to your web site and see what the total fee for MBA students really was. For the first time I realized that the tuition you are advertising for the program, and from which you are paying for campus services, is actually less than the total fees charged. This is (at best) misleading to students and a blatant attempt to avoid paying the campus its due share of MBA tuition revenues.

> You may appeal my decision to the President if you wish, but I will not forward your request with my approval.

To the provost:

The following table is directly from our full time MBA Program website:

How is this misleading?
You have approved every fee increase including the **100%** increase in fees in 2004 that were specifically discussed with you and the President in order to help offset the State budget cuts.
Our fee requests clearly lay out the costs they are set to recover and the distribution of fees between the part and full time programs. You have been fully aware of the school's budget model and the efforts and resources we have been

College Park Credit Hours	In-State Tuition	Out-of-State Tuition	Total Fees**	Total Tuition & Fees	
				In-State	Out-of-State
1	$803	$1,323	$1,058	$1,861	$2,381
2	1,606	2,646	1,585	3,191	4,231
3	2,409	3,969	2,122	4,521	6,081
4	3,212	5,292	2,639	5,851	7,931
5	4,015	6,615	3,166	7,181	9,781
6	4,818	7,938	3,693	8,511	11,631
7	5,621	9,261	4,220	9,841	13,481
8	6,424	10,584	4,747	11,171	15,331
9	7,227	11,907	5,468	12,695	17,375
10	7,227	11,907	5,995	13,222	17,902
11	7,227	11,907	6,522	13,749	18429
12	7,227	11,907	7,049	14,276	18,956
13	7,227	11,907	7,576	14,803	19,483
14	7,227	11,907	8,103	15,330	20,010
15	7,227	11,907	8,630	15,857	20,537
16	8,030	13,230	9,157	17,187	22,387

expending to improve student placement, etc. These have been encouraged by you and you have even complimented me on our successes.

If your goal is to induce me to step down by insulting me, you have succeeded. You will be receiving my letter vacating the dean's position as of August 31, 2007.

From the provost

I will look forward to receiving your letter.

I was furious. "What crap," I thought. I didn't need this and I wouldn't take it. I crafted my letter of resignation, showed it to my wife, and before sending it, I met with my academic department chairs and key administrators, gave them copies of my e-mails with the provost, and informed them that I would be resigning. They all were shocked and encouraged me to change my mind. I wouldn't and swore them to secrecy. I mailed my resignation to the provost and the president.

A few days later, I received the call (at home in the evening) from the president that I described at the start of this book. In the end, I would not resign at that time. My actual resignation would take place the following academic year. The provost also approved a somewhat modified fee proposal, and in a few months, everyone but me seemed to have forgotten the incident.

Our provost, on the other hand, would be leaving the campus in a few weeks to become the president of another university. Each year, at the end of the spring semester, it had become a tradition to have a dinner among the deans and the provost. We would be having our final dinner a few weeks after our argument. During dinner, we circled the table, with each dean giving a toast to the departing provost. I opened mine with the words, "I was thinking about how I could express my regard for him, but I decided to come anyway!"

A Parting Gift

I didn't expect that my last year at Smith would be very interesting. One year is not enough to start major new programs. I would take a less visible role on campus, essentially minding my own business. The comments of the deans as reported in my second five-year review had actually hurt my feelings, and I didn't want to have anything to do with them. I would restrict my travel and lay low. It didn't quite work out that way.

Every year or two Bob Smith would ask me the same question: "What can I do for the school that would really make a difference?" My usual response was: "Let me think about it for a month or two. I will get back to you."

In my final year, Bob again asked me "the question." I repeated the question at our bi-weekly Executive Committee Meeting. One department chair volunteered: "I'm not sure what we should do but whatever it is, it should help one area to leap forward above our competition."

This response started me thinking. The Smith Fellows Program was well in hand, so adding additional resources there would not be a great leap forward. Our Masters Programs required enormous resources, and anything that we added there wouldn't make a substantive difference. Our PhD program on the other hand, while very good, was relatively small (about one hundred students). Adding money there could make a big difference. It took me less than two months to create a proposal and sell it to Bob Smith and the university. In February 2008, we issued the following press release.

The Robert H. Smith School of Business at the University of Maryland today announced a $12 million PhD program initiative that will significantly enhance the school's ability to retain and attract the world's best and brightest students. The initiative, one of the most ambitious in the United States, increases annual doctoral stipends by 45 percent to $32,500 and provides research and travel support. Philanthropist and school namesake Robert H. Smith, a 1950 graduate, contributed $6 million toward the program, matched with funds from the University of Maryland and the business school.

The University is very grateful for Bob Smith's generosity. "The Smith School of Business is already internationally renowned, and this latest gift will give the students in it even greater opportunity," said University of Maryland President C.D. Mote Jr. "The University of Maryland is very fortunate to be collaborating on this initiative with Bob Smith. Together we are investing in a program that will significantly create educational opportunities for students planning a future in research."

"The Smith School is investing in its PhD program at a time when PhD programs are in crisis from a lack of sufficient resources, and business schools likewise suffer from a lack of talent to fill faculty positions," said Howard Frank, dean of the Robert H. Smith School of Business. "We hope to set an example by changing where the bar is set so ultimately, more and more talented students will consider entering an academic career."

The shortage of qualified business school faculty is so severe the Association to Advance Collegiate Schools of Business (AACSB) created a Management Education Task Force that, in its 2003 study Management Education At Risk, declared unless decisive action is taken to reverse declines in business doctoral education, academic business schools, universities, and society will be faced with an inevitable erosion in the quality of business education and research.

The Smith PhD Initiative includes a number of components designed to offer its doctoral students an unprecedented degree of compensation, resources and benefits. These include:

- **Super-stipends:** Incoming PhD candidates will benefit from a $32,500 annual stipend and subsequent $1,000 increases each succeeding year. Stipends for graduate students currently in the program will increase to average more than $25,000 per year. Additional stipends will be available for students who advance to candidacy and those who publish papers in A level research journals.

- **Dissertation support office:** A dedicated office with a professional editor and English-language training resources will assist the production of effective dissertations, teaching and communications training.
- **Research support:** Doctoral students will gain from year-round support to facilitate research and fifth-year fellowships for top students in order to increase research output and improve placement prospects.
- **Increased travel budget:** Students will be encouraged to more actively exchange knowledge and ideas with $1,500 per year available for travel and conferences
- **State-of-the-art facilities:** PhD students will enjoy a dedicated suite and offices in a newly completed wing of the Smith School's Van Munching Hall, opened January 2008. The PhD space was funded by William A. Longbrake, a 1976 doctoral alumnus now vice chair of Washington Mutual.

The Smith School's PhD program, ranked No. 6 in the United States and No. 13 in the world by the *Financial Times* (2008), has grown in both numbers and reputation over the past decade. The program attracts a global and very diverse group of PhD students. Currently 95 students represent 17 countries; about 69 percent are international and about 46 percent are women. Students regularly present papers at national as well as regional conferences and have papers accepted in major academic journals. In the past five years, 99 percent of Smith's Ph.D. students have been successfully placed directly after they graduate—about 80 percent as tenure-track assistant professors at accredited universities, and the rest as researchers in private or government organizations.

We coupled the press release with an e-mail campaign that delivered the release to thousands of professors at the top thirty business schools. No one in memory had made such a dramatic announcement. We were, if only for a little while, business school stars.

People

I worked with many wonderful people at the business school. The people I hired were super-competent and aggressive. The Smith environment was a superb training ground, and many left after a few years for promotions at other universities. In this way, my assistant dean for development became the vice president for advancement at a southern university. My associate dean for executive programs became deputy dean of a business school and after a few years, became president of a liberal arts college. Three of my senior associate deans became deans of business schools. (One of these was Maryland.)

Two of my staff—my assistant dean of finance and administration and my associate dean for undergraduate studies—stayed with me for the duration of my appointment. Both became allies, comrades, and friends. Without them, it would have been difficult to transform the school from mediocre to excellent.

My assistant dean for administration and finance tamed the financial management of the school. She replaced non-performing staff, hired a new crew, built financial controls, worked with me to build a sophisticated financial model of the business school, and managed the huge day-to-day transaction flow. She also managed the construction of the school's North Wing. Outside the business school, she put up with the obnoxious administrative university staff and absorbed insults directed at both her and me.

My associate dean for undergraduate studies joined me as an assistant dean early in my second year as dean. She too had a stiff spine and absorbed frequent insults from the university staff. She loved students and through a dedicated effort, helped transform the undergraduate program. She built a student club structure and an undergraduate student government. She was my partner in building the Smith Fellows Program and worked hard to recruit faculty and alumni mentors. She was my third eye and third arm, alerting me to university attempts to corrupt out standards and diminish our efforts and defending the program against these attempts.

I had four senior associate deans during my eleven years at Smith. All had been academics before they moved into the dean's office. They all worked hard to adapt to their new roles as managers, and I was fortunate because all were smart, good-natured, and well meaning. It was amusing to watch their attitudes toward faculty evolve from being one of them to viewing them as "them."

I built several significant staffs including information technology support, promotion, and development. All had fine managers.

Students are people too. In the beginning, our undergraduate students were a troubled lot, with most of my contact being negative. They would appeal to me when all of their other appeal routes were exhausted. I only reversed a single decision of my subordinates, and as I explained: "You are correct in your decision, but this person is so miserable that I don't want her around. She brings down other students, so give her what she wants and get her out of here as quickly as possible."

If there was a student waiting to complain, a parent was probably waiting in the wings. On one occasion, mother and daughter spent an hour complaining that my associate dean had insulted her by telling her, that if she couldn't take the pressure, maybe she should drop out of the business school. Throughout the hour, the twenty-one-year old student never stopped snuffling or crying. I was polite, but at the end, I couldn't resist. "You know what her problem is?" I asked the mother. When she answered "No," I responded: "YOU! Why are you here? She needs to grow up and handle her own problems."

My negative experience with undergraduates became positive as the students improved and became part of the new Smith School culture. After a while, the students loved the Smith School and I loved them. It was great fun to interact with these smart, mature individuals.

On the other hand, I found our MBA students to be demanding, self centered, and selfish. We had a few dedicated ones, but many students were critical of our efforts and would panic if a magazine ranking dropped. We had happy undergraduates but discontent MBAs. Balancing the MBAs were our PhD students who were treated well at Smith and responded by being very supportive of the school.

The campus outside of the Smith School was a different world. We would joke that we should build a moat around the school and populate it with alligators to keep outsiders away. (Outsiders probably joked that we should burn the Smith School down after building the moat.) Mutual distrust was the order of the day. After our first provost left to become president of another university, I could never count on the provost's words and actions to be honest and unbiased. The president said good things in public, but he didn't act to fix the system. I didn't trust the vice president for advancement who restricted my development staff's salaries and never came through with funding for the business school's development efforts, even though he got credit for our successes. In addition, the university was cavalier about the Smith School's donation prospects. They had no problem poaching our prospects to donate to other university projects even though we were forbidden to poach other's prospects. Business school alumni would be invited to serve on university boards and to support the president's pet projects without asking our permission.

University staff was the worst. Many were "lifers" who had joined academia for an easy life. They had joined the university when it was a mediocre state institution but hadn't adapted to the new Maryland. Consequently, they rebelled against the brash entrepreneurs from the business school. They slow rolled our projects, complained about our actions, and sabotaged our efforts. With the exception of a few people who were nasty to everyone, they smiled at us in public and sneered in private.

My colleagues, the other deans, were a mixed lot. There were a few good ones and from my view, a lot of bumpkins. While outwardly pleasant, they were a self-serving and hostile lot. I didn't see many leaders and was frequently surprised by their lack of management skills.

One dean vetoed a name change for one of our majors because "one of their programs might want to use that name in the future." It took two years to work out a very awkward compromise. We had to set up a university-wide major with the name we wanted. The Smith School could then offer a track under the overall major. It was a ridiculous arrangement but the only one possible. (Eight years later the offending college has still not offered that major.) That same dean told me "he nominated me for provost because then I would cut the business school's budget."

Others would say nice things to me and complain about me to the provost. I shared a few strategies for working around university policy. Within days, this was reported to the provost and I was admonished. The deans were jealous and uneducable. No matter how hard I tried to correct their beliefs about our lack of university funding, they were unable to see the truth. I could not count on them to honor past agreements, even if those agreements had been written and signed by their predecessors. The deans continued to hold the position that the business school had an unfair share of campus resources so they were entitled to violate and abrogate agreements.

One such violation was particularly egregious. We had executed an agreement with a college to teach specialized courses to our Shady Grove students. Money was transferred, but the other school never delivered the agreed number of courses. After continued complaints on my part, the provost made the matter worse by transferring additional business school money to the other college because, he said, "they need the money more than we did."

The End

I submitted my final resignation in August of my final year. This would give the university enough time to appoint a search committee for a new dean, conduct the search, and have a new dean in place when I departed. Because dean searches at Maryland are public, I informed the Smith Community of my resignation. This meant sending an e-mail to the staff and faculty and making many calls to members of my boards and supporters. I did not mention that I was serving on a one-year agreement that would end the following June no matter what I announced. I had to rebuff many pleas that I change my mind and stay. In reality, I was so fed up with the university that I wouldn't have stayed if given that choice. It was a quiet year. With the exception of the PhD initiative, I didn't start new projects.

Several of my senior staff declared that they would leave when I did. Two departed quickly, and I had to work to fill their slots. The major issue involved my replacement. The university selects deans through a public search process. Deans have little or no influence over the selection of their successors. I had a favorite candidate—my senior associate dean. I had recruited him from a major university and made him a department chair a few years later. After his appointment to senior associate dean, I had mentored him for a dean's position.

I thought he would make a fine dean but kept my views to myself. Once the other candidates were known, I gave detailed analyses of them and then declared my full support for him. I was elated when he was selected as the next dean of the Robert H. Smith School of Business.

As predicted by the president, I had a grand send off. There were receptions and parties. The president gave a fine speech about the wonderful things I had done for the school. My staff created a hilarious DVD entitled "Farewell to Dean Howard Frank." An undergraduate scholarship endowment was created in my name. Business school employees turned out in hordes to wish me well.

On the last day of June 2008, I left my dean's office for the last time. I had no regrets.

Chapter 9

What I Learned
(An Interview with
Dean Howard Frank)

What is your vision of the fundamental purpose of a business school?

The purpose of a business school falls within three main missions:

- Generating leading research—a business school needs to be on the forefront of creating new knowledge. This is one of the hallmarks of a true, major global business school.
- Creating great business leaders—a leading business school is one that creates business leaders who can leverage new tools, who can adapt to change, and whose thinking encompasses the world. These are the characteristics that will drive success in today's global, digital economy.
- Offering a return on investment—every one of our students will have a career that lasts many decades. Business schools need to think in terms of providing students a high return on investment, not just for the initial job upon graduation—but over the course of a career. Part of our responsibility is to teach students how to learn, adjust and adapt.

---

1   From an interview with Dean Howard Frank published in "Business School Leadership Strategies," edited by E. Fournier (Aspatore, Inc., 2006)

What are your goals for your school? How do they stem from/ correlate to the mission statement of the entire institution? How do you ensure you meet these goals?

Our goal at the Smith School is very simple—to be one of the great business schools of the world.

The extraordinary technological developments of the last decade are spawning new rules of economic engagement. The fundamentals of business are being transformed in every market, in every industry, in every nation. Those who understand how to create, manage, and leverage assets across boundary less organizations, using the tools of information technology and telecommunications, are the new barons of industry.

The impact of technology on the business environment has been felt in all aspects of business. Like businesses, business schools in the new millennium must transform their knowledge and research base, curricula, and modes of delivery. At the Smith School, we are in the midst of this transformation, with a vision of becoming a model for business education and knowledge advancement for the 21st century—and the next, great global business school.

What does it take? It means generating truly cutting-edge research, and creating great business leaders with students that go on to have fabulous careers.

The University of Maryland is a major research university and its goal is to become one of the top 10 public universities in the country, so the Smith School's goal of creating one of the truly great global business schools is entirely consistent and supportive of the university's mission.

How does management in the education field differ from managing in other industries?

Management in the education field is simultaneously both very similar and very different from management in other industries. The similarities lie within the fundamentals. For example, leadership is leadership. Vision is vision. Good management is good management. A key difference is that within a business school the primary productive resource—faculty—are quite independent of the institution. By default and by tradition, senior faculty members associate more with the profession than with the institution. Senior faculty members also have tenure—they don't have the traditional kinds of associations and accountability that an employee in a commercial organization does.

As a result, senior faculty members are very independent. Good management within a business school necessitates the alignment of faculty's interests with that of the institution and then creating a model where the faculty is working quite independently in a distributed fashion towards central goals. Every skill that you had before is required but you have to overlay on top of that a whole new set of constraints and operations.

Managing in a university environment is like being the CEO of a subsidiary of a large organization. You have many policies and constraints that fit within the parent organization and you must figure out how to meet the school's goals within that framework.

How do you measure success for your school? What benchmarks do you use?

Measuring success is fairly standard throughout the business education industry. All deans use a rather conventional set of objective benchmarks. We examine:

- Research ratings by department and for the school as a whole
- External rankings average for the school which does not have a lot of correlation with quality but it does have a fair amount of correlation with outside recognition
- Student completion and job satisfaction
- Student salaries and job histories
- Amount of donations and alumni giving

What are the most challenging aspects of being a dean for a business school? How do you overcome these?

I think the most interesting aspect of being dean is the fact that there are literally not enough hours in the day for the variety of demands on your time. You work with faculty. You work with students. You work with alumni. You externally represent the school. You work on strategy. You work on finance. If you divide up the day and ask, what is the job of the dean, you should be spending 50% of your time on each of these areas.

As a result, you need to be satisfied with being able to touch everything. You also need to be able to build management and administrative mechanisms that encourage the delegation of responsibility and management much like a conventional commercial organization.

At the Smith School we address this with a very unusual management structure—a parallel senior staff structure. I built a corporate-like environment within the business school, where talented senior executives, who are talented in their individual areas, work in parallel with the academic structure.

What qualities does a dean need to have long-term success?

The qualities a dean needs to build long-term success are the same qualities that any senior executive needs.

- The most important quality of any senior executive of a reasonably large organization is health and energy. You need to be able to run until you drop and then get up and do it again. If you don't have health, vitality and a high level of energy you can't get the job done.
- Vision and communications skills are also important
- Having a reasonable set of management skills, which are different than vision and leadership, are helpful.
- You also need a degree of luck. Given a choice between being lucky and being smart I'll take luck. You hear the expression

"people make their own luck" and it's true. Unlucky people don't see the opportunities that are randomly occurring. Lucky people see them and grasp some of them. You can't grasp all of them. You can't count on luck as being there exactly when you need it, which means you have to work hard in parallel with that. But if put yourself in enough opportunities there will be random things that occur that you can use.

How do you keep your edge as a dean of a business school? What resources do you find most useful in your position?

You keep your edge as dean by being an optimist. If you are a pessimist you shouldn't be a dean.

You also need a clear understanding of strategy and finance. You cannot drive the organization without an understanding of financial management.

What strategies or methodologies have you developed or use on a regular basis that make you a successful dean?

I am an entrepreneur. What does that mean? I like doing things that haven't been done before. I am happy when the environment is changing. So therefore I look at being dean as a wonderful intellectual challenge. Most people do not like managing in academia. In fact there is a misnomer that the words management and academia usually don't go together.

I always listen without killing the teller of bad news. It is vitally important you are able to understand reality—no matter how hard it is. As a leader, you may project the vision of everything as wonderful, but you have to be able to see it as it really is. You have to talk to the people who know—students, alums, and faculty—in the trenches. You have to listen to them because otherwise you will never understand what is really happening.

We have a successful continuous strategic planning process that enables us to link financial planning into strategic planning, so that our financial decisions are based on a vision of where we want to go.

How important is it to receive feedback from professors, students, and alumni? How do you get this feedback and how do you incorporate it?

You have to get feedback from your employees, not your managers. You have to hear what your managers are saying. It's not because your managers aren't believable. But every manager who works or reports directly to you has a vested interest in looking good and will filter information that comes to you.

You have to elicit feedback in a way that is not threatening, so you ask questions that are designed to encourage information but not put people on the spot. So for example, if I am trying to determine the caliber of faculty, I ask students what are their favorite classes, what are the best professors they've ever had. What are their least favorite classes? If I ask enough students I get a clear picture.

What is the best piece of advice you have ever received with respect to heading an institution?

The president of a university who had been dean of a business school before that told me to come see him for some tips when I told him I was becoming dean of a business school. He said, "Here's something that you should keep in mind. Everybody's going to ask you for money. And here's what you should do when they ask, you should say, 'that's very interesting,' as you put your arm around them and walk them to the door. 'Why don't you write it up?'"

This is the most memorable advice I have ever gotten.

How has the role of the dean changed in the past few years? How has the education industry changed? How has the business education industry changed in particular?

The role of a dean has become very much the role of a CEO—not the role of a caretaker, which was what the role of a dean was decades ago.

The educational industry is changing in remarkable ways. The development of continuous education models, part-time models, online models, and of global education are all in process. Business schools are all at the forefront and the role of dean in the educational business is tied to a market place that is changing faster than academia can possibly react to. Academia is a slow-moving, slow-reacting kind of business.

How do you expect the role of the dean to change in the coming years?

I expect the role of dean to be as dynamic and changeable as the past but more so. A dean needs to be an entrepreneurial, global manager.

If you could offer the three golden rules of being a dean for a business school, what would they be?

- Have a good sense of humor—if you don't you will hate it
- You have to be continuously optimistic
- You have to be aggressive—otherwise you will get run over by everybody in sight. You will get run over by your faculty, you will be run over by the university, you will be run over by the marketplace.

Thriving in the Educational Marketplace

How can you, as a school, strike the balance between a center for intellectual growth and a profitable institution that will be able to welcome others in search of such growth?

As a market-driven, commercial manager, I don't believe you can operate without a profitable financial structure. Creating a high value generating business school requires financial wherewithal, and this should be the top priority. Create a profitable, fast-growth institution and then you can create intellectual growth and capital.

How does a business school make money? What are the areas that generate the most revenue? What ancillary areas develop significant revenue streams (apparel licensing, sports TV/radio fees, etc.)?

Our most significant revenue streams come from our educational programs and in particular from our graduate education—MBA, part-time MBA, Executive MBA, and non-degree programs.

What are the most expensive elements of operating a business school (payroll, facilities, technology, etc.)?

The most expensive element of operating a business school is payroll. For example, the Smith School's budget this year is roughly $65 million and our payroll is over $30 million of that. The next most expensive element of operating a business school includes a group of items that have comparable costs of about $2–3–4 million each annually—running offices such as the MBA office or career management center, technology, facilities and marketing communications.

What factors go into determining tuition?

The Smith School is a state school so the university via the Board of Regents sets undergraduate tuition. The Board of Regents is appointed by the governor and is influenced by the State legislature so it is as much a political decision as one involving meeting the needs of the university, and is intensely political and has nothing to do with the cost of actually providing education. The business school's graduate tuitions are market based but must be approved by the Regents.

What factors drive it up or down?

I have never seen tuition go down! If you look at the various costs built into running an institution, faculty salaries have been going up on average of about 4–5 percent annually for some time. Other costs that contribute to tuition increases are tied directly to inflation, while others such as heating and building costs have increased much faster than inflation. These are the same factors that drive any business's operations. But they only go up—they don't go down.

How do you build the school's endowment? How is this money then invested?

The way we build the school's endowment is by asking our alumni to support various projects for the school. The money then goes into an overall university endowment fund and is invested by professional managers. The monies donated for the business school are dedicated to us and, of course, can be used only for the purposes for which they were given.

When I first came to the Smith School we had a $6.5 million endowment. We have had a substantial number of gifts over the last five to seven years totaling approximately $100 million with close to half having gone into endowment.

Financial support from our alumni, including transformational gifts from Leo Van Munching, Jr. '50, and Robert H. Smith '50, have allowed the school to make a giant leap into a leadership position in the digital economy. The Smith School was named in honor of Mr. Smith in 1998, when he provided an endowment of $15 million, the school's largest gift ever. Since then the school's stature and size have undergone a dramatic transformation with the addition of world-class research centers, top-flight faculty and increased student quality.

What are the long-term goals for this money, in general terms?

You can't think of managing an endowment in general terms. You have to think in specific terms to meet the agreement between you and the donor and the school.

How do you go about fundraising—setting goals, executing, how important is fundraising and how do you set forth a successful plan?

Successful fundraising entails thinking in terms of what is truly important strategically for the school. The answer in general terms is pretty obvious:

- People
- Facilities
- Wherewithal to deliver first-class education

As far as people, there are two kinds—faculty and students. For faculty you want endowed positions. For students you want scholarships. We are constantly investing in facilities. Since I've arrived here we will have built over $60 million in facilities and so a part of our fundraising goal is to pay for those facilities.

The distribution between these areas is determined by discussions among our senior managers with the number one priority given to what we think it is realistic to generate in each area and then to what the school's needs are.

Fundraising is essential. If you look at a major public business school there is no difference between it and a private business school in terms of cost structure. If I am going to compete for faculty I am going to compete for the best faculty and they can go to either a public or private school. We are going to pay them the same as if they went to the top private institution. If I am going to build a building the fact that it's sitting on University of Maryland ground doesn't make it any cheaper to build than if it were sitting on Harvard or Wharton ground. Nobody cares about public versus private when we are heating the building.

So if you look at the life of any major school, fundraising is one of the critical ways of achieving goals. There are really only three ways you can get money. You can earn it. You can steal it. Or someone can give it you. And since we are not in the business of stealing money someone must give it to us or we have to earn it. So how do you go about fundraising? The execution of it is actually quite systematic and sophisticated—it is marketing. You build a marketing plan. You look at who your potential donors are. You actually meet with them. You put a marketing organization—which in a university setting is a development organization—in place and call on people continuously for years and build individual relationships.

What role do the trustees play in the financials of your school?

The Board of Regents has a very significant role. They set an environment that is even more important than the specific financial role they play in setting tuition levels. They are key influencers in how people view public education.

From a financial standpoint, what do you believe constitutes a successful institution?

I think there are only two directions—up or down. I don't believe in flat. Flat is a non-viable direction. If you look at the pressures of managing a business school—you always need more, you always need better. This all costs more money. With money I can solve all of the other issues. Mine is definitely a commercial private sector view of the educational marketplace.

I think that the most important thing to recognize is that if you are at the upper end of the business school environment there really are no significant differences between public and private schools other than some of the constraints in which you operate. We have a procurement structure that's specified by the state. So that's definitely a constraint. We have certain things like undergraduate tuition that are set much lower than the cost of providing education versus private schools which can recover their costs with tuition. So there really are differences, but the actual operations of the schools, for first-class public and private schools, are really technically the same. So I don't think in terms of public schools as our competition. Our competition is the best business schools in the country.

What drives the recognition/popularity of an institution (for the public, for prospective students, etc.)? What about your institution, in particular?

- History—part of what drives recognition of an institution is having been around a long time and having a strong alumni base.
- Marketing
- Producing world-caliber research in volume—that generates academic respect which then goes into generating public recognition

Chapter 10

Frank Conclusions—
A Jaundiced View of Academia

The University Environment

- The university is an archaic structure with positions reporting to positions but hardly anyone taking direction.
- Management rarely exists. That's why they call "managers" "administrators." In the commercial world, administrators push paper but do not manage. When you call someone an administrator, you haven't said a nice thing. In the academic world, the term "manager" is considered a derogatory term.
- Academic financial planning and management is an illusion. This fact is made even more bizarre in public universities, where the state can act to reduce university budgets without regard to earlier plans, promises, or institutional needs.
- People management is a tautology. It is neither practiced nor appreciated.
- The system protects and rewards the weak and punishes the strong.
- The business school is an oasis of capitalism in a desert of socialism.
- There are two cultures at work. A democratic faculty culture without management and an administrative culture without management or democracy.
- Nearly all view the environment as a zero sum game, so it's in others' interests for you to have less.
- No one outside your school has your best interests in mind. Others will not consider your interests at all when acting on their own agendas.

- A written agreement is worthless. A verbal agreement does not exist. A deal sealed by a handshake is an act of lunacy.
- You have a better (although still slim) chance of having deals honored by your peers than your superiors.

Personal Behavior

- Ethics and integrity are an abstraction. People will agree to something to stop you from talking about it. They will have no intention of honoring the agreement.
- A deal is a deal until it is convenient for the other party to ignore it.
- Trust at your peril. It's better to not trust, verify, and be prepared to strike back.
- Don't base premises on promises. A promise is simply a means to get you to drop the subject. When it comes up again, the promise will turn out to be an illusion.
- Most people think that it is perfectly proper to steal unlicensed software from Microsoft because "Microsoft already makes too much money."
- Constant vigilance is a good approach.

Managing Relations

- At some point, you will be blindsided and hit. When you get hit, you must immediately hit back.
- Hitting back harder is worth a pound of prevention. It may keep you from being hit a second time. However, prepare to be disliked or hated for striking back since this is not part of the academic culture.
- Trap, rope, and hogtie; don't try to reason and convince.
- Instead of fighting the impossible battle, delay and obfuscate.
- Being a team player is a good idea, but recognize that most people are not on your team.
- You are not paranoid. They are out to get you.

- It's difficult to separate sheer incompetence from laziness or malevolence.
- Your opposition will follow almost any approach other than confrontation.
- Don't expect a call back if the topic is unpleasant.
- They will promise to send it to you but never will.
- The system tolerates rude behavior. Politeness is not a standard.
- Speaking out, eccentricity, "venting" etc. etc. are all condoned JUST SO LONG AS IT'S NOT confrontational in a way that would alter the environment.
- Maladjusted people have a home here.
- Character assassination is tolerated.
- If you allow it to happen, it will happen. And it will happen to YOU.

Managing Change

- It's difficult to start new good things but nearly impossible to kill existing bad things.
- Strategy is planning until Friday night.
- Change is the enemy. When you want to change something, there will be at least a small group who react as if the change meant the end of the world.
- Because changing the system is virtually impossible, find the holes and seams in the system and work through or around them.
- Be prepared for new rules to be created that will thwart your efforts to work around the seams and holes in the system. These rules will be especially crafted to prevent your actions but will be portrayed as "always existing" and "nothing new at all."
- Radical change, if thought to be radical, will be rejected out of hand. You will be asked to benchmark what other (peer) schools are doing with the notion that if they aren't doing it, you shouldn't be either.
- Major changes must be made in small, almost invisible steps.

- The status quo, and inertia, its principal tool, is divine.
- The only way to move the business school quickly forward is to force other parts of the campus in the right directions. They will not go quietly and you will end up with many adversaries and enemies.
- Prepare to be disliked.

University and Business School Finances

- Most business schools (especially publics) are considered cash cows by campus administration and receive less than the average university financial support. However, to compensate, they have greater than the average number of students.
- The larger business schools have found ways to generate substantial additional revenues to support themselves. Few if any faculty or staff outside the business school understand this, and they think that the business school is benefiting at their expense.
- Success in revenue generation will be rewarded (i.e., "no good deed goes unpunished") by reductions elsewhere in your budget.
- People will ask you for money (with a straight face) for totally absurd and unreasonable things. They will try to take if from you at the end of the academic year without asking.
- Budgets are a fiction. You will be assessed unbudgeted costs at year-end without consultation or planning. Nonetheless, you will be expected to operate deficit-free even though no one can give you an accounting of your total expenses.
- One way to measure success is by the size of the deficit you can generate without being fired.
- Promises for future money will not be kept. This, however, will not prevent others from expecting you to honor all of your pledges.
- If someone from another unit sends you money by mistake, keep it. He or she would not return it to you if it had been your mistake.

- A non-business school committee will not grant you money.
- Don't try to audit the books. They will not balance.
- Don't ever expect an accounting of any other unit's expenses, even if this is part of a cooperative deal and promised to you.

Other Deans

- Don't try to confuse them with the facts. This merely prolongs the conversation.
- Most deans appear to be nice people, but "niceness" can be a façade.
- No matter what they say, they don't have your interests in mind, but they hate the fact that you don't have theirs.
- All deans expect equality, except when it means reducing their resources.
- If you protect your own interests, you will be considered a bad campus citizen. You will be perceived to be a mercenary. This perception will not be changed no matter how generous you are.
- There are enough competing interests among groups of deans that the only viable approach is to change nothing.
- Any act of graciousness on your part will be viewed as suspicion. Therefore, you must develop a somewhat obvious hidden agenda that can be deduced and accepted.
- Deals you make will be forgotten—either by the deans you make them with or their successors. Their successors will have no written records or understandings of the original terms, even if you carefully documented them at the time.

University Governance

- University policy exists because it exists.
- Facts are irrelevant.
- Faculty Senates are the home of the inept and the den of the terminally boring.

- If you want to kill something, refer it to a committee of faculty or staff who will study your proposal in great depth and then tell you why it is a bad idea.
- When senior administrators don't want you to do it, they will refer you to a committee.
- Committees, when evaluating a proposal, will ask you for "benchmark" data; i.e., which of your peers are doing what you are proposing. Being the first in anything is not a positive attribute.
- Even if the committee agrees with you, the member appointed to document the agreement can delay it indefinitely. In this case, there is no recourse since the subject will always be referred back to the one responsible for documentation.
- If you have an idea that is perfect for your school but not applicable to others, it will be rejected because everyone should be treated equally. If you try to apply it to everyone, it can't be passed because you must gain consensus first.
- Consensus cannot be achieved on any issue worthy of seeking consensus.
- If it's your idea (as a business school dean), it must be a bad idea because you don't have the other school's interests at heart. The fact that they don't have yours is not relevant.

The Development (Funds Raising) Process

- The university directs development and pays for it except when it is for the business school, in which case it expects to direct development but not pay for it.
- Your leads are your leads but can be reassigned when convenient.
- Your major, most visible alumni will be recruited to serve on university initiatives and will be asked to donate to other projects. If you object, you are not a team player.
- Objecting to poaching of your prospects is like preemptive jury challenges—you get a certain number and then are out of luck.

- Poaching is a cardinal sin—except when it is done to the business school or the president does it.
- The central staff is chosen because of their lack of imagination and initiative. The role of their senior administrators is to keep them this way.
- If you invest your own resources to expand your development activities, the university will reduce its support by at least an equal amount.
- When asking for future support, you will get unequivocal statements about the importance of what you are doing and its impact on the university. The support will never arrive.

Time Management

- There will be frequent opportunities to be forthright and candid in public. Doing so will save you the time from serving on many university committees.
- Some university committees (e.g., the Finance Committee) have deans on them. If asked to serve on such a committee, don't be impressed. It is merely for show. When serving, ask a lot of good questions. You will not be asked back.
- The phrase, "That's an interesting idea; why don't you write it up?" can save you all sorts of time.
- If you don't have a hidden agenda, get one. Don't propose what you really want since you will not get it. Propose something far more extreme and settle for your desired outcome.

The Faculty

- A faculty member is special kind of human. "Not everybody can get along with faculty."
- The more you do for a faculty member, the more he or she will expect.
- There is an inverse relation between faculty support and faculty satisfaction.

- Business faculty members are frequently the highest paid faculty on campus. Whatever their salary, they think it is inadequate. (Example: faculty member who wants the extension of his summer support guarantee three years from now because he is becoming an associate editor of a journal and is worried about his "productivity.")
- Most deans think of and refer to their faculty as children.
- Whatever teaching loads and faculty support a school has, faculty and department chairs will report better conditions at other schools. The deans of those other schools will not confirm these reports.
- Aberrant individuals will be accepted, tolerated, or ignored, even if they are really crazy.
- Crazy faculty will be assigned to teach undergraduate courses, where they can drive their students crazy too and do the most harm.
- Really incompetent faculty members have permanent homes with little stress or pressure. When they retire, their colleagues may even vote to grant them "emeriti" status.
- Most faculty members come to top business schools to do research. They consider teaching to be overhead and believe that university life would be perfect (except for salary, parking, secretarial support, travel accounts, and other support factors) if there were no students.
- The expectations of junior business faculty are directly proportional to the quality of the schools from which they graduate.

The Staff

- Staff satisfaction decreases with length of time in service.
- There are two kinds of staff: "gung ho dynamos" and the terminally bored.
- The university performance appraisal and pay policies are designed to treat these two classes as indistinguishable from one another.

- The best way to retire on the job is to work in an academic department in a staff position. The senior faculty or department chair will be reluctant to impose reasonable performance standards, and the junior faculty will accept the status quo as normal.
- There are some reasonable staff in other parts of the campus. Find them and make them your allies, but do not expect to find them in positions of authority.
- University staff (e.g., personnel, academic affairs, accounting) make and administer university policy but do not have the faintest idea about the impact of their rules on the operations of the academic units.
- Don't expect numbers given to you about anything to be the same whether given to you by two different people or by the same person on two different days. In addition to being incorrect, at least one set of numbers will not even add to 100% or to the listed total.
- It's more important to staff that things be done according to policy than be done the right way. Policy will always trump efficiency.
- Staff hired from the non-academic world will have a difficult time adjusting to the academic world. They will have to accept irrational administrative policies, inept personnel management systems, archaic business processes, and lack of drive and incentive in their colleagues from other parts of the campus.
- A staff meeting will never take less than an hour to accomplish what should be a twenty-minute job.

University Administrators

- The president is treated as a godlike figure. After a while, he or she believes that this is normal and true.
- The president of the university has no idea of what goes on in the bowels of the organization.
- No one is willing to tell the president "no" or to reveal the ugly truths about the operations of the institution.

- The president makes decisions based on how it might look on the front page of the local newspaper. The right thing to do is a second order consideration.
- The provost is the number two administrator on campus. It is a miserable job because the only real powers of the position are the ability to say no and the ability to transfer money from one school to another. The provost, like any group executive, does not make things happen but can keep them from happening.
- Provosts feel perfectly entitled not to honor the agreements of their predecessors.
- A good provost can be a great asset to an aggressive dean by not getting in the dean's way.
- Deans must be patient with provosts because the provost's job is to prevent the business school from having more than other schools. Therefore, most provosts and business school deans maintain an uncomfortable truce, especially since the provost can unilaterally punish the business school without regard to fairness, equity, due process, or other accepted standards of behavior.
- Most business school deans think and speak of their provosts as the evil enemy. A dean expects that if he supports a particular issue, his provost will be against it (and vice versa.)
- You can be sure that when the provost interprets the application of university policy with respect to the business school, the result will penalize the school.
- The provost's staff will be highly negative towards the business school and block the school at any opportunity.

The Rankings

- Business schools are blessed and cursed by a variety of magazine and business newspaper rankings.
- Virtually all agree that the contents of these rankings lack substance and in some cases are outrageous or ridiculous. Nonetheless, virtually all deans proudly announce positive movements in any one ranking.

- Many rankings ask deans to rank other schools even though they have no idea what other schools are doing. This does not prevent them from expressing their opinions.
- A dean's opinion of a school is related to its nearness to his or her school in the rankings. That is, the closer two schools are to one another, the lower the respective opinions of their deans about one another. The same rule applies to schools geographically close to one another. Most are comfortable in saying nice things about Wharton or Harvard, which is why, Wharton and Harvard remain highly ranked.
- Students, faculty, and alumni treat rankings as gospel, even when they know better.
- Many of the publishers of business school rankings are more interested in changes in the rankings among schools than in the fairness or accuracy of the rankings. Change creates sales.
- Schools lie or distort data they report to the trade press for use in rankings. Many deans do not see an ethical problem in this.

Students

- Students choose schools based on location, rankings, finances, and their abilities to be admitted. Performance of the university's sports teams is another important factor.
- Once admitted, student expectations and satisfaction are highly correlated with their ability to get a job.
- You can't get undergraduates to read the text, and you cannot please the average MBA student no matter what you do or no matter what tuition you charge.
- Students would enjoy business school a great deal more if they didn't have to take courses, go to class, take tests, or do homework.
- To attract top students, you must promise them the world. After they enroll, they will become disappointed because no one can deliver the world.

- Once you do a poor job in an area, most students will never perceive that you are doing a good job no matter what else you do or how much better you become.
- The better you do in an area, the greater the expectation students will have for future improvements and the greater their disappointment that you are not delivering.
- Business students have a difficult job perceiving the academic institution as a business and have an even more difficult job in correlating their expectations for service with tuition paid.
- Every applicant to the business school believes that he or she would make a perfect business student, regardless of their grades or qualifications. They understand and appreciate the need for standards but expect special consideration for themselves.

Alumni

- Athletics and academics are co-equal in the memories and value systems of alums.
- Dissatisfied graduates can make excellent alums since their expectations have been set so low.
- Alums are proud that the school has high standards but expect special consideration for their own children and relatives when they fail to meet admission standards.

Parents

- Parents want their children to stand on their own feet but have no compunction about calling the dean when their students don't get the grades or treatment they think they deserve.
- Parents blame the school when their child is too drunk to attend class.
- Every parent thinks that his or her child is a special case and deserves special consideration.

- Parents emasculate their children by fighting their battles for them but expect that administrators and faculty should treat their children as grownups.

Appendix

The First Smith School Strategic Plan

The Robert H. Smith School of Business University of Maryland ascent to the top the plan for 1998–2003 vision and strategy

Executive Summary

The Robert H. Smith School of Business is implementing a strategy that will distinguish itself as one of the nation's best schools for business learning and knowledge advancement. To achieve this, the School has two strategic foci. The first is across-the-board elevation of the quality of our academic areas and centers through research, teaching and outreach. The second is differentiation around the creation, management and deployment of knowledge and information. By the year 2003:

- the School will be viewed nationally and internationally as the center of excellence for business research and skill acquisition in the area of knowledge and information management;
- graduates of the School will be differentiated because of their immersion in a learning environment that prepares them for future leadership, and stimulates skill development in creating, growing and managing, business organizations of the 21st century;
- the School will have developed cross functional expertise in telecommunications, electronic commerce, supply chain man-

agement, financial engineering, entrepreneurship, global business and knowledge management, and the management of technology, by drawing on its core competency in knowledge management and information systems;

- the School will have expanded partnerships with other colleges of the University of Maryland to seize and respond to cross-disciplinary opportunities and requirements in the marketplace;
- the school will achieve national recognition in highly targeted outreach programs (executive education, management development and entrepreneurship);
- the School's status in the national rankings will be augmented and solidified with the goal of advancing in the ranks of the nation's most highly rated business schools;
- resources and infrastructure in the school will be selectively enhanced to remedy deficiencies and achieve balanced excellence in each program;
- the resources available to the school will enhance faculty and staff recruitment, development and retention, ongoing innovation and quality improvement in our programs, and a supportive and stimulating work environment for all members of the Robert H. Smith School of Business community.

This plan outlines tactics in six strategic areas needed to achieve the school's vision. These are research excellence, academic program distinctions, cross-functional education and research, information technology as a core competency, marketing the school, and increasing resource support.

VISION

"With the advent of the information revolution—or the third industrial revolution (call it what you will)—skills and knowledge have become the only source of sustainable long-term competitive advantage ... For more than a century, the world's wealthiest human being has been associated

with oil. ... But today, for the first time in history, the world's wealthiest person is a knowledge worker ... The nation's most profitable companies are those with a lock on some form of knowledge."
—Lester Thurow, *Harvard Business Review*, September–October, 1997, pp. 96–97

The stature of the Robert H. Smith School of Business has advanced dramatically over the last decade. Several measures support that assertion:

- the MBA program has been recognized in the top 25 national rankings three times in the last decade (*US News*);
- the MBA program is very attractive to potential graduates—it has tripled in size over the last decade while simultaneously enhancing student quality;
- the quality of our full-time MBA students is ranked as 16th in the country in terms of student selectivity (*US News*, 1998);
- the undergraduate program is ranked 20th in the country (*US News*, 1997);
- several of our academic areas are recognized among the top ten in their respective fields (entrepreneurship, logistics, management science, and information systems);
- the recently completed University of Maryland Graduate Program Review ranked the business MBA and Ph.D. degrees in the "established excellence" category;
- demand for our graduates is unprecedented—the number of on-campus corporate recruiters serviced by the Robert H. Smith School of Business Career Center doubled between Fall 1996 and Fall 1997;
- our centers are increasingly the "partner of choice" to all segments of the region's business community.

Given its recent successes, the Robert H. Smith School of Business is poised to join the ranks of the most eminent business schools in the country. How should a business school advance knowledge and prepare its graduates for the newly created economic structures of the next century? The answer hinges on identification of the primary source of wealth in the foreseeable future. As Lester Thurow aptly states, it will reside in intangible assets—knowledge and information.

In a recent *Harvard Business Review*, Philip Evans and Thomas Wurster predict that "Over the next decade, the new economics of information will precipitate changes in the structure of entire industries and in the ways companies compete" (*HBR*, September–October 1997, p. 71). Those who understand how to create, manage, and leverage intangible assets across boundaryless organizations, using the tools of information technology and telecommunications, will be the next barons of industry. New market forces and organizational forms have emerged. They create non-traditional opportunities for competitive advantage, new sources of value and methods of asset valuation, new strategies for reaching and retaining customers with unprecedented reach to global markets, the preeminence of intellectual property, national and international economic policy and ethical dilemmas never encountered before, and emergent centers of global excellence without regard for countries' traditional economic power base.

The rapidity of technical and knowledge changes, and the volatility of sources of market advantage will require the future leaders of global businesses to be highly adaptive and receptive to new and complex information. These accelerating changes also necessitate development of new theoretical models for understanding, evaluating, and affecting the efficient and fair practice of business in the "third industrial revolution."

These are the challenges for business schools of today yet, in general, the schools are lagging. For the most part their students emerge with inadequate preview and preparation for this new order, and on the research and application front they have been slow to develop models of knowledge-based business processes, e.g., financial accounting models for intangible assets (*Wall Street Journal*, November 3, 1997), value chain deconstruction in the age of direct connectivity (Evans and Wurster, *HBR*, 1997), or a global system of intellectual property rights (Thurow, *HBR*, 1997). The challenge to business schools is to catch up and deliver in these key areas. This is precisely the vision of the Robert H. Smith School of Business: to advance business thinking and education for this new economic order.

The Robert H. Smith School of Business—The Next Five Years

One way of articulating a vision for the next five years is to take a snapshot of the school, as we wish it to be, in the year 2003. The key elements are as follows:

- The school, through its portfolio of programs (research, curricula, and outreach), will be viewed nationally and internationally as a center of excellence for the advancement of business knowledge and critical competency in the management of knowledge and information. It will be known for targeted sources of academic distinction that support the overarching theme of knowledge and information management (e.g., entrepreneurship, management of technology, telecommunications and information technology, supply chain management, electronic commerce, etc.);
- the school, as part of a strong research university with a strategy of inter-unit collaboration among business, engineering and the sciences, will have expanded partnerships with other colleges to capitalize on opportunities and requirements in the marketplace;
- graduates of the School will be differentiated because of their immersion in a learning environment that prepares them for future leadership, and stimulates skill development in creating, growing and managing, business organizations of the 21st century;
- the school's status in the national rankings will be augmented and solidified with the goal of ranking among the nation's top programs at both undergraduate and graduate levels;

- resources and infrastructure in the school will be selectively enhanced to remedy deficiencies and achieve balanced excellence in each program;
- the school will achieve national recognition in highly targeted outreach programs (executive and management development, entrepreneurship);
- the resources available to the school will enhance faculty and staff recruitment, development and retention, ongoing innovation and quality improvement in our programs, and a supportive and pleasant work environment for all members of the Robert H. Smith School of Business community.

Strengths of the Robert H. Smith School of Business

Is this vision realizable? The answer depends on the distance between where we are today versus where we want to be, and the extent to which present advantages can be leveraged into the future vision. Accordingly, how do we view the present strengths of the Robert H. Smith School of Business in relation to this vision?

The established reputation for outstanding faculty research and Ph.D. program excellence in several areas of the Robert H. Smith School of Business can be leveraged into high quality research and graduate programs, provided there is leadership and support for the new foci of research, and recruitment of outstanding faculty in these areas.

The national rankings of the MBA program already garner attention for our programs, attracting outstanding students and some measure of corporate recognition. The rankings are not a single monolithic concept but are comprised of specific numerical parameters which reflect the success of the educational programs and which will be affected by the school's strategies and action plans. For example, the five highest components of the *US News and World Report* MBA rankings are: academic reputation (25%), average GMAT (16.25%), corporate reputation with recruiters (15%), median starting base salary (14%) and percent employed three months post-graduation (12.25%).

These parameters represent reasonable educational goals that are addressed by the school's strategies. With regard to these elements of the rankings, we currently place as follows in *US News, 1998*: academic reputation (#36), average GMAT (#17), corporate reputation (#44), median starting base salary (#39) and percent employed three months post-graduation (#21). Therefore, we can achieve among the very best by improving our recognition with deans and recruiters (through the quality of faculty and academic programs) and by increasing the job attractiveness of our graduates. Since having quality academic programs is related directly faculty quality, adding senior professors and endowed chairs will be crucial to moving upwards in the ratings.

The undergraduate rankings and innovative cross-functional "boutique" programs (TQ, Business Honors, College Park Scholars) increasingly attract outstanding students and external recognition for the programs. Several cross-functional programmatic strengths are already emerging within the Robert H. Smith School of Business and with other units on campus (e.g., logistics and supply chain management, telecommunications, international business) and can be readily leveraged into broader programmatic emphases that are consistent with the vision.

Our centers have achieved significant regional and even national recognition for their sources of excellence, suggesting that the prospects for national stature and enhanced business activities for the centers are very promising. The school is characterized by highly entrepreneurial thinking and a tradition of innovation, such as revenue sharing initiatives, differential tuition, geographic diversification, and flexible degree portfolios responsive to the needs of different market segments. This tradition will facilitate the transformation into a new operating model.

The school has a large and successful alumni base and corporate network, with the prospect of significant private giving. This year's record, as the best fundraising year ever culminating in the naming gift by Robert H. Smith, suggests momentum as we enter the active phase of the comprehensive campaign.

There are barriers to achieving the vision and, unless removed, they hamper our ability to move forward. We are at a disadvantage in competing for outstanding new faculty hires with the top schools because of too few distinguished endowed chairs and research professorships. A central determinant of rankings in *US News* is placement indicators. However, our MBA and undergraduate placement measures do not match the caliber of the student body. We will need specific, targeted efforts to improve these indicators. The external community's general impression of the Robert H. Smith School of Business (referring here to both academic and corporate observers) under-represents true program quality. The school must increase its promotional activities to achieve the recognition that it currently deserves and to then raise the level of its recognition to the level that the school will achieve in the next five years.

Strategies to Realize the Vision

The school will design and implement a new business school model around the creation, management, and deployment of knowledge and information. This includes the following cross-cutting content innovations in our curriculum, drawing on virtual research groups within the school and linkages with other disciplines on campus:

- Telecommunications
- Management of technology
- Electronic commerce
- Financial engineering
- Supply chain and logistics management
- Global business and knowledge management
- Entrepreneurship

The school will introduce innovative undergraduate and MS cross-functional programs to attract top quality students and to enhance placement through market responsiveness to uniquely trained students. Internal (students) and external (alumni and members of the business community) stakeholders will be closely engaged to provide input and feedback around design of the programs. Included among the programs is a new accelerated MS in business for life sciences and computer sciences undergraduates, the recently approved College Park Scholars program on Business, Wealth, and Society designed jointly with Economics, and an undergraduate citation in entrepreneurship open to all sophomores from across campus. These distinctive programs will: (a) attract high quality undergraduates; (b) retain strong graduating seniors for an additional year on campus to broaden and enhance their career prospects through a combined degree with business; and (c) attract a broader recruiter portfolio to the business school because of the availability of a new "breed" of graduates with joint degrees, thus enhancing placement prospects for *all* business graduates.

We will hire and retain top tenure-track faculty, with a key goal of building excellence in emerging thematic emphases. Targeted hires will accelerate the school's progress in implementing and obtaining distinction through the strategic shift to a business school focused on knowledge and information management. Using the opportunity enabled with the Robert H. Smith endowment, "stars" will be hired in areas of strategic need. Initially, stars will be sought for the information systems, and the PepsiCo Chair in Marketing. Our goal is to add seven endowed chairs and twelve endowed research professorships to the faculty. These endowed chairs and professorships provide funds which supplement faculty salaries thereby enabling the school to hire exceptional faculty who are at the top of their fields. In addition to increased salaries, such positions are a significant mark of academic distinction and are crucial to top faculty recruitment and retention.

Undergraduate and MBA placement statistics will be strengthened through an organized campaign to attract corporate recruiters, and through programs to enhance career mentoring for both graduate and undergraduate students. We will provide customized referral of graduates and utilize multiple channels for placement including advisory boards, a "Career Associates" program and target well placed alumni in companies that fit the desired profile. Promoting the new concentrations and school's focus on the information revolution will increase the attractiveness of graduating students.

External and corporate recognition for the Robert H. Smith School of Business will be increased through strategic marketing of the sources of distinction in the school—the new business school model and corporate-oriented programs that advance core competencies in the creation and management of knowledge and information. The school will implement a comprehensive strategy to engage alumni and the business community and to market its sources of distinction, including hiring a senior marketing director to deploy the strategy. It will increase academic and professional activities and communicate these activities with public relations activities targeted at deans and recruiters.

The school will increase strategically targeted financial support for top quality Masters and Ph.D. students. At the Masters level, financial aid is critical to preserve the quality of the student body and, thus, an important determinant of the rankings. To attract outstanding Ph.D. students and maintain the vibrancy and excellence of our graduate research program, the financial support package offered to prospective Ph.D. students will be enhanced.

We will improve our stature in the rankings by focusing on the previously stated goals of enhanced placement and student career skills, strategic marketing, and leadership in curriculum innovation. Continuous improvement processes are part of the culture of the Robert H. Smith School of Business and will be used to achieve critical improvements in students' learning and development experiences. These focused improvement activities are targeted, coincidentally, at the areas with the greatest potential for upward movement in our ranking components, and will result in improved and solidified rankings.

We will generate additional revenues through innovative programs leveraging existing strengths and launching new partnerships with other units on campus and elsewhere, to support implementation of the above strategies. We will pursue the Robert H. Smith School of Business goals for the comprehensive campaign with vigor.

The campaign objectives for the Robert H. Smith School of Business are endowment funds for faculty chairs and professorships, the MBA Career Center, student scholarships and financial aid, and the Center for Technology, all of which are central to realizing the vision for the Robert H. Smith School of Business. "Star" researchers cannot be hired without the funds and status of endowed chairs and professorships; placement results at the MBA level, a critical input factor for rankings, are enabled with the resources of an endowed center; attraction of a top quality and diverse student body depends on the availability of financial support at the undergraduate and graduate levels; and the Center for Technology provides the technical means for supporting the content shift of the Robert H. Smith School of Business to a focus on managing knowledge and information.

External funds are also essential to solve the school's shortage of space, a situation that will significantly limit the school's ability to advance forward and attract top students and faculty unless remedied. With endowment and other sources of support, the Robert H. Smith School of Business plans to add a wing to Van Munching Hall, to accommodate the space requirements for its expanding programs and client usage. The primary uses for the new wing will be additional classrooms, expanded executive and management development facilities, larger Career Management services at both undergraduate and graduate levels, and faculty offices to accommodate the growth in the school's size.

Tactics for Academic Years 1998/9 to 2002/3

Research   To support research excellence, the RHS School
Excellence   will create an infrastructure that enables and stimulates
prolific, top quality research.

Action goals include:
* guaranteed full 20% summer research support for all productive faculty
* reduced course load for junior faculty at least once pre-tenure
* recruitment of 7 new endowed chairs thanks to the RHS endowment and the PepsiCo chair. Areas include Information Systems, Accounting Systems, and Marketing (PepsiCo Chair in Consumer Research)
* the award of 12 research professorships to outstanding researchers who are current and future members of the School
* attraction of the most promising new faculty at all levels through competitive recruitment packages
* retention of productive faculty through aggressive salary actions
* post-tenure reviews and feedback for tenured faculty
* meaningful 3-year reviews and contract decisions for junior faculty
* active mentoring and support of junior faculty in each area to position them for promotion and tenure
* attraction of top quality Ph.D. students through more lucrative fellowships/scholarships and minimal teaching requirements

- expanded infrastructure for information technolo-gy-related research including hardware, labs, soft-ware, professional and para-professional support, implemented through a Center for Information Technology

Academic program

To move forward in the rankings, the RHS School will sustain its educational distinctiveness, innovation and high quality.

Action goals include:

- launching and marketing an innovative MBA program that incorporates cross-functional business solutions and flexible program options; reflects stakeholder (business and student) input in design
- enhancing the input quality and placement successes of the Masters population by targeted increases in scholarships and financial aid
- improving the quality of the UG population through improved pedagogy, boutique programs that attract top students state-wide and nationally, and selective admissions
- improving pedagogy through teaching enhancement interventions and IT support of learning.
- shoring up permanent faculty/student ratios to en-hance the quality of teaching and learning

Cross-functional strategy

To distinguish itself in research and education, the RHS School will develop cross-functional expertise in knowledge and information management and flows.

Action goals include:

- creation of mechanisms to support team-teaching without penalty

- establishment of research incentives (e.g., a targeted research pool) to launch and sustain collaborative, inter-disciplinary research
- hiring faculty who can add research and teaching strength beyond a single functional area
- offering extended funding opportunities for selected research activities that are particularly well aligned with the school's strategy
- targeting new elective development in cross-functional content areas

IT as core competency

To enhance its distinction as a leader in knowledge and information management and flows, the RHS School will aggressively use information technology tools.

Action goals include:
- establishment of Center for Information Technology, including infrastructure for support of IT-related research (see above)
- selective development and delivery of distance education activities in its academic, certificate and executive education programs
- expansion of the portfolio of executive and management education programs to focus on IT content, clientele, and advanced IT learning tools
- selective development of new courses, simulations and applications in non-IS areas that highlight IT, e.g., accounting systems, finance trading floor and simulations, hi tech marketing management
- support of the integration of information technology into the curriculum of a wide variety of UG and Masters courses

Marketing the RHS School

To achieve the recognition it deserves, the RHS School will engage in intense and focused activities to publicize its distinctions and expand its alliances with the business and corporate world. Action goals include:

- creation of area advisory boards to advance business partnerships, research opportunities, financial support, and student placement
- seeding research centers in selected areas that exploit and advance faculty expertise in the area, and serve as a focal point for external recognition and business partnerships
- systematically integrating all marketing efforts across areas, programs and centers into coherent themes and image
- expanding presence in the Baltimore *and* Northern Virginia region, especially through the Office of Executive Programs (Baltimore) and the Dingman Center (Northern Virginia)
- enhancing placement outcomes (see measures) by targeted partnerships with well-paying corporate recruiters matched to student profile, and through interventions to improve student job search skills

Resource support

To realize the above strategies, the RHS School will generate the requisite human and financial resources. Action goals include:

- hiring non-tenure track faculty as "super" teachers across all programs to assume a higher teaching burden, and provide course load relief to faculty
- establishing higher teaching loads for faculty no longer active in research

- raising additional resources to fully finance new wing to Van Munching Hall
- leveraging current programs into new programs and revenue streams that enhance the brand name through high delivery quality, yet add substantial new resources given costs, e.g., Baltimore, Accounting MS, Life Sciences/Computer Sciences joint MS, Center for Management Excellence
- maximizing the returns from new programs and activities through creative financing and partnership arrangements e.g., computer leasing, new self-based revenue approach as new model for campus
- creatively using RHS naming gift for endowed chairs and strategic priorities of RHS School
- raising additional new private funds to support faculty research, center launches and student financial support
- utilization of more efficient delivery (e.g., distance education) and management (e.g., outsourcing and leasing) mechanisms
- receipt of additional faculty and staff lines from the university
- introduction of new sources of revenue while minimizing the "net new" burden, e.g., through higher market pricing of existing programs, repackaging courses into certificate programs or concentrations, and modularized delivery to facilitate scheduling flexibility.